A NATION OF IMMIGRANTS

Books by John F. Kennedy

A NATION OF IMMIGRANTS

THE BURDEN AND THE GLORY
  (edited by Allan Nevins)

TO TURN THE TIDE
  (edited by John W. Gardner)

THE STRATEGY OF PEACE
  (edited by Allan Nevins)

PROFILES IN COURAGE

WHY ENGLAND SLEPT

A NATION OF

Revised and Enlarged Edition

Harper & Row, Publishers

John F. Kennedy

IMMIGRANTS

Introduction by ROBERT F. KENNEDY

New York and Evanston

PICTURE CREDITS: Research and editing by Sam Holmes and Charles Reynolds. (1) From *Nova Britannia* by Robert Johnson (London, 1609), courtesy of the Rare Book Division, New York Public Library. (2) From *Ausfuehrliche Historie der Emigranten oder vertriebenen Lutheraner aus dem Ertz-Bissthum* Salzburg (Leipzig, 1732–34), courtesy of the Rare Book Division, New York Public Library. (3) From *Your America Day-by-Day* by Clark Kinnaird; copyright 1950, King Features Syndicate, Inc. (4) From *White Servitude in Colonial South Carolina* by Warren B. Smith, courtesy of University of South Carolina Press. (5) and (6) Courtesy of the New-York Historical Society, New York City. (7) From *To the Golden Door* by George W. Potter, courtesy of Little, Brown and Company. (8) The Bettmann Archive. (9) Courtesy of the Library of Congress. (10) Culver Pictures, Inc. (11) The Bettmann Archive. (12) *Harper's Weekly*, June 6, 1863. (13) Courtesy of the Nebraska State Historical Society. (14) Courtesy of the Minnesota Historical Society. (15) Courtesy of the Weyerhaeuser Company. (16) Brown Brothers. (17) Courtesy of the Museum of the City of New York. (18) Courtesy of the Library of Congress. (19) Brown Brothers. (20) and (21) Lewis W. Hine, courtesy of George Eastman House. (22) Culver Pictures, Inc. (23) Courtesy Library of Congress. (24) Lewis W. Hine, courtesy of George Eastman House. (25) and (26) Brown Brothers. (27) Lewis W. Hine, courtesy of George Eastman House. (28) Brown Brothers. (29), (30), (31) and (32) Courtesy of U.S. Immigration and Naturalization Service. (33) Courtesy of Polish Museum of America, Chicago. (34) Arnold Genthe, courtesy of the California Historical Society. (35) Courtesy of U.S. Immigration and Naturalization Service. (36) Brown Brothers. (37) Lewis W. Hine, courtesy of George Eastman House. (38) From the Jacob A. Riis Collection, courtesy of the Museum of the City of New York. (39) Courtesy of the New York Public Library. (40) and (41) United Press International. (42) Wide World Photos, Inc. (43) From *The Herblock Book*, Beacon Press, 1952, courtesy of Herbert Block. (44) Ernst Haas, Magnum Photos. (45) From *The Decisive Moment* by Henri Cartier-Bresson, Magnum Photos, published by Simon & Schuster, Inc. (46) United Press International. Prints for (5), (18) and (23) from John Houseman's film *Voyage to America*, courtesy of United States Commission, New York World's Fair.

LIBRARY OF CONGRESS CATALOG CARD NUMBER: 64–7830

CONTENTS

A group of illustrations follows page 18.

INTRODUCTION

I know of no cause which President Kennedy championed more warmly than the improvement of our immigration policies. Our attitude toward the immigrant has gradually matured to a full appreciation of the contribution he can make and has made to American life. Much of the story of that development is set forth in this book. But recent years have witnessed a legislative lag.

Every forward step in immigration legislation since World War II bore the John F. Kennedy imprint: the Displaced Persons Act and the Refugee Relief Act, which he sponsored while in Congress; the 1957 bill to bring families together, which he led to passage in the Senate; and the comprehensive reform of our law which he recommended to Congress as President.

In 1958, while the fight for the 1957 amendments was still fresh, he published his first edition of this book. It was deliberately designed to provide those who were unfamiliar with this aspect of our history with an appreciation of the enormous contributions to American life made by immigrants. He felt that this understanding was essential to any future effort to eliminate the discrimination and cruelty of our immigration laws.

When President Kennedy sent his historic message to Congress calling for a complete revision of the law, he decided it was also time to revise the book for use as a weapon of enlightenment in the coming legislative battle.

He was working on the book at the time of the assassination. It was decided that it should be published posthumously. This legacy should not be denied those committed to the battle for immigration reform.

President Kennedy's interest in the immigrant and in the law governing his admission to the United States sprang from many sources. He was himself only two generations removed from an immigrant. On his sentimental visit to Ireland in June of 1963, he stood at the spot from which Patrick Kennedy embarked, and said:

When my great-grandfather left here to become a cooper in East Boston, he carried nothing with him except a strong religious faith and a strong desire for liberty. If he hadn't left, I would be working at the Albatross Company across the road.

For fourteen years, in the House and in the Senate, he represented Massachusetts, which has the highest percentage of foreign nationality groups of any state in our country. President Kennedy met with them, in their homes and factories, at their picnics and cultural events. He admired their heritage and their determination to succeed. A student of history, President Kennedy understood the fruitful interplay between the immigrants and the nation they adopted. They must be given full credit for changing America from a colony to a leader of the free world, from a predominantly agricultural economy to a highly diversified, highly skilled industrial complex.

Our attitude toward immigration reflects our faith in the American ideal. We have always believed it possible for men and women who start at the bottom to rise as far as their talent and energy allow. Neither race nor creed nor place of birth should affect their chances.

As I stated before the House Judiciary Subcommittee on Immigration and Nationality in July, 1964, it is my conviction that there are few areas in our law which more urgently demand reform than our present unfair system of choosing the immigrants we will allow to enter the United States. It is a source of embarrassment to us around the world. It is a source of anguish to many of our own citizens with relatives abroad. It is a source of loss to the economic and creative strength of our nation as a whole.

There is no reason to believe that anything has happened to change the relation between America and its immigrants. The number of people who wish to come here today is much smaller than it was in the nineteenth century. But their aspirations are the same. Their need is as great. The contribution they can make is, if anything, even greater.

In this book, President Kennedy tells us what immigrants have done for America, and what America has done for its immigrants. It is one of the dramatic success stories of world history. I am very happy that this book is being reissued now, so it can stand as a testament to a cause President Kennedy cherished, and which we should carry on.

ROBERT F. KENNEDY

A NATION OF IMMIGRANTS

CHAPTER 1

A Nation of Nations

On May 11, 1831, Alexis de Tocqueville, a young French aristocrat, disembarked in the bustling harbor of New York City. He had crossed the ocean to try to understand the implications for European civilization of the new experiment in democracy on the far side of the Atlantic. In the next nine months, Tocqueville and his friend Gustave de Beaumont traveled the length and breadth of the eastern half of the continent —from Boston to Green Bay and from New Orleans to Quebec— in search of the essence of American life.

Tocqueville was fascinated by what he saw. He marveled at the energy of the people who were building the new nation. He admired many of the new political institutions and ideals. And he was impressed most of all by the spirit of equality that pervaded the life and customs of the people. Though he had reservations about some of the expressions of this spirit, he could discern its workings in every aspect of American society—in politics, business, personal relations, culture, thought. This commitment to equality was in striking contrast to the class-ridden society of Europe. Yet Tocqueville believed "the democratic revolution" to be irresistible.

"Balanced between the past and the future," as he wrote of himself, "with no natural instinctive attraction toward either, I could without effort quietly contemplate each side of the question." On his return to France, Tocqueville delivered his dispassionate and penetrating judgment of the American experiment in his great work *Democracy in America*. No one, before or since, has written about the United States with such insight. And, in discussing the successive waves of immigration from England, France, Spain and other European countries, Tocqueville identified a central factor in the American democratic faith:

All these European colonies contained the elements, if not the development, of a complete democracy. Two causes led to this result. It may be said that on leaving the mother country the emigrants had, in general, no notion of superiority one over another. The happy and powerful do not go into exile, and there are no surer guarantees of equality among men than poverty and misfortune.

To show the power of the equalitarian spirit in America, Tocqueville added: "It happened, however, on several occasions, that persons of rank were driven to America by political and religious quarrels. Laws were made to establish a gradation of ranks; but it was soon found that the soil of America was opposed to a territorial aristocracy."

What Alexis de Tocqueville saw in America was a society of immigrants, each of whom had begun life anew, on an equal footing. This was the secret of America: a nation of people with the fresh memory of old traditions who dared to explore new frontiers, people eager to build lives for themselves in a spacious society that did not restrict their freedom of choice and action.

Since 1607, when the first English settlers reached the New World, over 42 million people have migrated to the United States. This represents the largest migration of people in all recorded history. It is two and a half times the total number of people now living in Arizona, Arkansas, Colorado, Delaware, Idaho, Kansas, Maine, Montana, Nevada, New Hampshire, New Mexico, North Dakota, Oregon, Rhode Island, South Dakota, Utah, Vermont and Wyoming.

Another way of indicating the importance of immigration to America is to point out that every American who ever lived, with the exception of one group, was either an immigrant himself or a descendant of immigrants.

The exception? Will Rogers, part Cherokee Indian, said that his ancestors were at the dock to meet the *Mayflower*. And some anthropologists believe that the Indians themselves were immigrants from another continent who displaced the original Americans—the aborigines.

In just over 350 years, a nation of nearly 200 million people has grown up, populated almost entirely by persons who either came from other lands or whose forefathers came from other lands. As President Franklin D. Roosevelt reminded a convention of the Daughters of the American Revolution, "Remember, remember always, that all of us, and you and I especially, are descended from immigrants and revolutionists."

Any great social movement leaves its mark, and the massive migration of peoples to the New World was no exception to this rule. The interaction of disparate cultures, the vehemence of the ideals that led the immigrants here, the opportunity offered by a new life, all gave America a flavor and a character that make it as unmistakable and as remarkable to people today as it was to Alexis de Tocqueville in the early part of the nineteenth century. The contribution of immigrants can be seen in every aspect of our national life. We see it in religion, in politics, in business, in the arts, in education, even in athletics and in entertainment. There is no part of our nation that has not been touched by our immigrant background. Everywhere immigrants have enriched and strengthened the fabric of American life. As Walt Whitman said,

These States are the amplest poem,
Here is not merely a nation but
a teeming Nation of nations.

To know America, then, it is necessary to understand this peculiarly American social revolution. It is necessary to know why over 42 million people gave up their settled lives to start anew in a strange land. We must know how they met the new land and how it met them, and, most important, we must know what these things mean for our present and for our future.

CHAPTER 2 ⚑

Why They Came

⚑

Little is more extraordinary than the decision to migrate, little more extraordinary than the accumulation of emotions and thoughts which finally leads a family to say farewell to a community where it has lived for centuries, to abandon old ties and familiar landmarks, and to sail across dark seas to a strange land. Today, when mass communications tell one part of the world all about another, it is relatively easy to understand how poverty or tyranny might compel people to exchange an old nation for a new one. But centuries ago migration was a leap into the unknown. It was an enormous intellectual and emotional commitment. The forces that moved our forebears to their great decision—the decision to leave their homes and begin an adventure filled with incalculable uncertainty, risk and hardship—must have been of overpowering proportions.

Oscar Handlin, in his book *The Uprooted*, describes the experience of the immigrants:

The crossing immediately subjected the emigrant to a succession of shattering shocks and decisively conditioned the life of every man that survived it. This was the initial contact with life as it was to be. For many peasants it was the first time away from home, away from the safety of the circumscribed little villages in which they had passed all their years. Now they would learn to have dealings with people essentially different from themselves. Now they would collide with unaccustomed problems, learn to understand alien ways and alien languages, manage to survive in a grossly foreign environment.

4

Initially, they had to save up money for passage. Then they had to say good-bye to cherished relatives and friends, whom they could expect never to see again. They started their journey by traveling from their villages to the ports of embarkation. Some walked; the luckier trundled their few possessions into carts which they sold before boarding ship. Some paused along the road to work in the fields in order to eat. Before they even reached the ports of embarkation, they were subject to illness, accidents, storm and snow, even to attacks by outlaws.

After arriving at the ports, they often had to wait days, weeks, sometimes months, while they bargained with captains or agents for passage. Meanwhile, they crowded into cheap lodginghouses near the quays, sleeping on straw in small, dark rooms, sometimes as many as forty in a room twelve by fifteen feet.

Until the middle of the nineteenth century the immigrants traveled in sailing vessels. The average trip from Liverpool to New York took forty days; but any estimate of time was hazardous, for the ship was subject to winds, tides, primitive navigation, unskilled seamanship and the whim of the captain. A good size for the tiny craft of those days was three hundred tons, and each one was crowded with anywhere from four hundred to a thousand passengers.

For the immigrants, their shipboard world was the steerage, that confined space below deck, usually about seventy-five feet long and twenty-five feet wide. In many vessels no one over five and a half feet tall could stand upright. Here they lived their days and nights, receiving their daily ration of vinegar-flavored water and trying to eke out sustenance from whatever provisions they had brought along. When their food ran out, they were often at the mercy of extortionate captains.

They huddled in their hard, cramped bunks, freezing when the hatches were open, stifling when they were closed. The only light came from a dim, swaying lantern. Night and day were indistinguishable. But they were ever aware of the treacherous winds and waves, the scampering of rats and the splash of burials. Diseases—cholera, yellow fever, smallpox and dysentery—took their toll. One in ten failed to survive the crossing.

Eventually the journey came to an end. The travelers saw the coast of America with mixed feelings of relief, excitement, trepidation and anxiety. For now, uprooted from old patterns of life, they found themselves, in Handlin's phrase, "in a prolonged state of crisis—crisis in the sense that they were, and remained, unsettled." They reached the new land exhausted by lack of rest, bad food, confinement and the strain of adjustment to new conditions. But they could not pause to recover their strength. They had no reserves of food or money; they had to keep moving until they found work. This meant new strains at a time when their capacity to cope with new problems had already been over-burdened.

There were probably as many reasons for coming to America as there were people who came. It was a highly individual decision. Yet it can be said that three large forces—religious persecution, political oppression and economic hardship—provided the chief motives for the mass migrations to our shores. They were responding, in their own way, to the pledge of the Declaration of Independence: the promise of "life, liberty and the pursuit of happiness."

The search for freedom of worship has brought people to America from the days of the Pilgrims to modern times. In our own day, for example, anti-Semitic and anti-Christian persecution in Hitler's Germany and the Communist empire have driven people from their homes to seek refuge in America. Not all found what they sought immediately. The Puritans of the Massachusetts Bay Colony, who drove Roger Williams and Anne Hutchinson into the wilderness, showed as little tolerance for dissenting beliefs as the Anglicans of England had shown to them. Minority religious sects, from the Quakers and Shakers through the Catholics and Jews to the Mormons and Jehovah's Witnesses, have at various times suffered both discrimination and hostility in the United States.

But the very diversity of religious belief has made for religious toleration. In demanding freedom for itself, each sect had increasingly to permit freedom for others. The insistence of each successive wave of immigrants upon its right to practice its religion helped make freedom of worship a central part of the American creed. People who gambled their lives on the right to believe in their own God would not lightly surrender that right in a new society.

The second great force behind immigration has been political oppression. America has always been a refuge from tyranny. As a nation conceived in liberty, it has held out to the world the promise of respect for the rights of man. Every time a revolution has failed in Europe, every time a nation has succumbed to tyranny, men and women who love freedom have assembled their families and their belongings and set sail across the seas. Nor has this process come to an end in our own day. The Russian Revolution, the terrors of Hitler's Germany and Mussolini's Italy, the Communist suppression of the Hungarian Revolution of 1956, and the cruel measures of the Castro regime in Cuba—all have brought new thousands seeking sanctuary in the United States.

The economic factor has been more complex than the religious and political factors. From the very beginning, some have come to America in search of riches, some in flight from poverty and some because they were bought and sold and had no choice.

And the various reasons have intertwined. Thus some early arrivals were lured to these shores by dreams of amassing great wealth, like the Spanish conquistadors in Mexico and Peru. These adventurers, expecting quick profits in gold, soon found that real wealth lay in such crops as tobacco and cotton. As they built up the plantation economy in states like Virginia and the Carolinas, they needed cheap labor. So they began to import indentured servants from England, men and women who agreed to labor a term of years in exchange for eventual freedom, and slaves from Africa.

The process of industrialization in America increased the demand for cheap labor, and chaotic economic conditions in Europe increased the supply. If some immigrants continued to believe that the streets of New York were paved with gold, more were driven by the hunger and hardship of their native lands. The Irish potato famine of 1845 brought almost a million people to America in five years. American manufacturers advertised in European newspapers, offering to pay the passage of any man willing to come to America to work for them.

The immigrants who came for economic reasons contributed to the strength of the new society in several ways. Those who came from countries with advanced political and economic institutions brought with them faith in those institutions and experience in making them work. They also brought technical and managerial skills which contributed greatly to economic growth in the new land. Above all, they helped give America the extraordinary social mobility which is the essence of an open society.

In the community he had left, the immigrant usually had a fixed place. He would carry on his father's craft or trade; he would farm his father's land, or that small portion of it that was left to him after it was divided with his brothers. Only with the most exceptional talent and enterprise could he break out of the mold in which life had cast him. There was no such mold for him in the New World. Once having broken with the past, except for sentimental ties and cultural inheritance, he had to rely on his own abilities. It was the future and not the past to which he was compelled to address himself. Except for the Negro slave, he could go anywhere and do anything his talents permitted. A sprawling continent lay before him, and he had only to weld it together by canals, by railroads and by roads. If he failed to achieve the dream for himself, he could still retain it for his children.

This has been the foundation of American inventiveness and ingenuity, of the multiplicity of new enterprises, and of the success in achieving the highest standard of living anywhere in the world.

These were the major forces that triggered this massive migration. Every immigrant served to reinforce and strengthen those elements in American society that had attracted him in the first place. The motives of some were commonplace. The motives of others were noble. Taken together they add up to the strengths and weaknesses of America.

The wisest Americans have always understood the significance of the immigrant. Among the "long train of abuses and usurpations" that impelled the framers of the Declaration of Independence to the fateful step of separation was the charge that the British monarch had restricted immigration: "He has endeavoured to prevent the population of these States; for that reason obstructing the Laws for the Naturalization of Foreigners; refusing to pass others to encourage their migrations hither, and raising the conditions of new Appropriations of Lands."

CHAPTER *3*

Waves of Immigration—
the Pre-Revolutionary Forces

Immigration flowed toward America in a series of continuous waves. Every new migration gathered force, built momentum, reached a crest and then merged imperceptibly into the great tide of people already on our shores.

The name "America" was given to this continent by a German mapmaker, Martin Waldseemüller, to honor an Italian explorer, Amerigo Vespucci. The three ships which discovered America sailed under a Spanish flag, were commanded by an Italian sea captain, and included in their crews an Englishman, an Irishman, a Jew and a Negro.

Long before the colonies were settled, the Spanish and French explorers left evidences of their visits on great expanses of the American wilderness: the Spanish in a wide arc across the southern part of the country, from Florida, where they founded St. Augustine, our oldest city, in 1565, through Texas and New Mexico, to California; the French, up and down the Mississippi and Ohio River valleys. Spanish influence can be seen today in our architecture, in the old missions, in family names and place names such as Los Angeles, San Francisco and Sacramento; the French influence is apparent in many towns and cities still bearing the names of the original settlements, such as Cadillac, Champlain and La Salle.

The first wave of settlement came with the colonists at Jamestown in 1607 and at Plymouth in 1620. It was predominantly

English in origin. The urge for greater economic opportunity, together with the desire for religious freedom, impelled these people to leave their homes. Of all the groups that have come to America, these settlers had the most difficult physical environment to master, but the easiest social adjustment to make. They fought a rugged land, and that was hard. But they built a society in their own image, and never knew the hostility of the old toward the new that succeeding groups would meet.

The English, the numerical majority of the first settlers, gave America the basic foundation of its institutions: our form of government, our common law, our language, our tradition of freedom of religious worship. Some of these concepts have been modified as the nation has grown, but the basic elements remain. Those who came later built upon these foundations. But America was settled by immigrants from many countries, with diverse national ethnic and social backgrounds.

There were both indentured servants and profit-seeking aristocrats from England. There were farmers, both propertied and bankrupt, from Ireland. There were discharged soldiers, soldiers of fortune, scholars and intellectuals from Germany. The colonies welcomed all men, regardless of their origin or birth, so long as they could contribute to the building of the country. The Dutch settled Nieuw Amsterdam and explored the Hudson River. The Swedes came to Delaware. Polish, German and Italian craftsmen were eagerly solicited to join the struggling Virginia colonists in Jamestown. The Germans and Swiss opened up the back country in Pennsylvania, New York, Virginia and the Carolinas. French Huguenots took root in New England, New York, South Carolina and Georgia. The Scots and the Irish were in the vanguard that advanced the frontier beyond the Alleghenies. When Britain conquered Nieuw Amsterdam in 1664, it offered citizenship to immigrants of eighteen different nationalities.

At one time it seemed the continent might ultimately divide into three language sections: English, Spanish and French. But the English victories over the French and the purchase of territories held by the French and Spanish resulted in the creation of an indivisible country, with the same language, customs and government. Yet each ethnic strain left its own imprint on the new land.

Thus the very name of our country, "The United States of America," was borrowed from "The United States of the Netherlands." Many "typical American" activities are Dutch in origin. The immigrants from Holland brought to this country ice-skating, bowling, many forms of boating and golf (which they called *kolf*); they gave us waffles, cookies and that staple of the American menu, the doughnut (originally *kruller*). To our folklore they contributed the figure of Santa Claus and his reindeer, and the many tales of the Hudson Valley. Examples of their architecture can still be seen on the banks of the Hudson today.

French colonial immigration had two main sources. The Protestant Huguenots came here in considerable numbers after persecution resumed as the result of the revocation of the Edict of Nantes in 1685. The Catholic "Acadians" came here after their exile from Nova Scotia in 1755 when that land fell under British rule.

The Huguenots settled in the larger trading towns of New England, later spreading down through Pennsylvania and Virginia, and in South Carolina. A Huguenot family presented Faneuil Hall, a shrine of American liberty, to the city of Boston. Many of the beautiful houses which make Charleston so picturesque today were built originally by Huguenots.

The Acadians, relatively few in numbers, scattered mostly along the Eastern seaboard. But a colony of them settled in Louisiana, along the bayous to the west and north of New Orleans. They were relatively isolated, and as they grew in number, they kept their language, their customs, their faith and folklore, even abiding by the Napoleonic Code rather than English law. Today, sometimes known as "Cajuns," they provide one of the most distinctive ethnic elements on the American scene.

During and after the French Revolution of 1789, French musicians, dancing masters, tutors and wigmakers, once employed by the now deposed aristocrats, added a touch of grace to the homespun life of the new nation. They introduced the French art of cooking, as well as the cotillion, the waltz and the quadrille.

French-Spanish émigrés from the West Indies made New Orleans into a great cultural and social center. The first opera to be given in America was produced in that city. The only major American city built according to a systematic plan, Washington, D.C., was designed by the French Army engineer Major Pierre Charles L'Enfant.

The early Swedes, too, made their contribution to American culture—in particular, the knowledge of how to build houses from squared-off timbers. This structure was later to become the mark of the frontier, where it was known as the log cabin.

Over two thousand Jews came to this country in pre-Revolutionary days. Most were from Spain or Portugal. Some established themselves in the Dutch colony of Nieuw Amsterdam, after winning recognition of their right to trade, travel and live in the colony from Peter Stuyvesant. Others settled in Newport, Rhode Island, then a thriving center of the maritime trade. Many prospered as merchants in the West India trade, which included sugar, rum and molasses. The oldest synagogue in the United States, built in 1763, is located in Newport, Rhode Island.

Among the earliest settlers in Pennsylvania were Welsh farmers who came here for economic reasons and out of a desire to revive Welsh nationalism. In the years 1683–99, they were augmented by Welsh Quakers who came to escape religious persecution. Their presence is reflected by such place names as Bryn Mawr and Radnor, and in the sturdy farmhouses of the area, still standing after almost three hundred years.

The pre-Revolutionary Irish immigration is usually referred to as Scotch-Irish, since it consisted largely of Scots who had settled in Ireland during the seventeenth century.

These were the frontiersmen, ideally suited by their previous environment and experience to spearhead the drive against the colonial frontiers. They pushed out almost at once to the edge of the wilderness in Pennsylvania, Maryland and Maine, and down the Great Valley to the Carolina Piedmont. Through them, Presbyterianism became a powerful force on the frontier. The Scotch Presbyterians founded many institutions of higher learning, beginning with Princeton in 1746.

In 1683 thirteen German families arrived in Philadelphia. They were the forerunners of a substantial migration from Germany. With them there also came Swiss, Alsatians, Dutch and Bohemians. By the eve of the Revolution there were over 100,000 German immigrants and descendants of German immigrants living in the United States. They constituted the first numerical challenge to the hitherto predominantly English population.

Some were Pietists, Moravians and Mennonites, sects in some ways similar to the Quakers. They found in William Penn's colony a sympathetic climate in which they could practice their beliefs without interference.

Those of their descendants who live today in and around Lancaster County, Pennsylvania, are known as the "Pennsylvania Dutch." They have made of their land a model of conservationist farming. Nearly three hundred years after they first broke ground, their land is as fertile and productive as they found it. They built the first Conestoga wagon, a vehicle which was to prove immensely useful to the settlement of the West.

Other German immigrants were members of other religious groups, such as the Amish and the Dunkards, who like to be known as "the plain people." They have changed little in their folkways and religious practices. They still wear their traditional clothing and follow traditional customs, providing, like the Cajuns, a picturesque addition to the American scene.

Although there was no large-scale Italian immigration before the Revolution, there were many Italians prominent in American life. As early as 1610, craftsmen were brought from Italy by the colony of Virginia to start a glass trade. Later, others came and planted vineyards. Georgia invited them to organize a silk industry.

In all the large cities there were Italian doctors, merchants, innkeepers and teachers. They wandered everywhere as traveling musicians, held concerts and established music schools. Our first sculptors and our first interior decorators were Italian.

Although predominantly Catholic, the Italians had their own counterpart of the Puritans, the Waldensians. They were an independent sect from the Piedmont, in the north of Italy, who were invited by the Dutch colonial government to form settlements here. Some 167 of them accepted, and in 1657 they were brought to the New World to settle a tract of land set aside for them by the Nieuw Amsterdam government.

Poles, too, were present in pre-Revolutionary America. Originally, they, too, came at the invitation of the Dutch. Most of them were farmers, but some settled in what is now New York City, where one of them, Dr. Alexander Kurcyusz (Curtius), a prominent physician, founded the first Latin school. Pre-Revolutionary America also included Greeks, Russians and other Slavs, immigrants from Southeastern and Eastern Europe.

During the Revolutionary War itself, men came from many other lands to help the new nation. Two Poles helped turn the tide toward victory. Thaddeus Kosciusko, a young engineer, offered his services early. He became an aide to General Washington and a major general in the engineers. His plans are credited with winning the Battle of Saratoga, a turning point in the war. Count Casimir Pulaski rose to the rank of general, fought heroically at Brandywine, Trenton and in other decisive engagements. He organized his own Polish Legion, ultimately giving his life to the new nation when he died as a result of a wound received at the Battle of Savannah. A German, Baron Friedrich Wilhelm von Steuben, did more than anyone else to shape the raw recruits into a disciplined army. A Frenchman, Marquis de Lafayette, has become something of an American folk hero for his part in the Revolution. He took a leading part in the campaign that led to the defeat of Cornwallis at Yorktown. The service of another Frenchman, Count de Rochambeau, who recruited over four thousand French volunteers, was almost as great.

Between a third and a half of the fighting men of the Revolutionary Army were of Scottish or Scotch-Irish descent. Many of those at Valley Forge were German.

A Pole of Portuguese-Jewish origin, Haym Salomon, risked his life to gain vital intelligence for the American cause. A Scotch-Irish immigrant, Robert Morris, helped finance the war.

Four signers of the Declaration of Independence were immigrants of Irish birth: Matthew Thornton, James Smith, George Taylor and Edward Rutledge. The great doctrine "All men are created equal," incorporated in the Declaration by Thomas Jefferson, was paraphrased from the writing of Philip Mazzei, an Italian-born patriot and pamphleteer, who was a close friend of Jefferson. Mazzei compiled the first accurate history of the colonies, which he wrote in French so that the European nations would be able to appreciate the political, social and economic conditions that characterized the new world.

A gravestone in the Shenandoah Valley of Virginia reads: "Here lies the remains of John Lewis, who slew the Irish lord, settled in Augusta County, located the town of Staunton and furnished five sons to fight the battles of the American revolution." Statements like this not only speak eloquently of the contribution of one Irish family, but represent the sacrifices of many immigrants to this country even before it had won its independence.

CHAPTER 4

Waves of Immigration— the Post-Revolutionary Forces

American independence, the spreading westward of the new nations, the beginnings of economic diversification and industrialization, all these factors gave immigration in the nineteenth century a new context and a new role. The gates were now flung open, and men and women in search of a new life came to these shores in ever-increasing numbers—150,000 in the 1820's, 1.7 million in the 1840's, 2.8 million in the 1870's, 5.2 million in the 1880's, 8.8 million in the first decade of the twentieth century. And, as the numbers increased, the sources changed. As the English had predominated in the seventeenth and eighteenth centuries, so the Irish and Germans predominated in the first half of the nineteenth and the Italians and East Europeans in the last part of the nineteenth and the early part of the twentieth centuries. Each new wave of immigration helped meet the needs of American development and made its distinctive contribution to the American character.

THE IRISH

The Irish were in the vanguard of the great waves of immigration to arrive during the nineteenth century. By 1850, after the potato famine, they had replaced England as the chief source of new settlers, making up 44 percent of the foreign-born in the United States. In the century between 1820 and 1920, some four and a quarter million people left Ireland to come to the United States.

They were mostly country folk, small farmers, cottagers and farm laborers. Yet they congregated mainly in cities along the Eastern seaboard, for they did not have the money to travel after reaching shore. Few could read or write; some spoke only Gaelic.

The Irish were the first to endure the scorn and discrimination later to be inflicted, to some degree at least, on each successive wave of immigrants by already settled "Americans." In speech and dress they seemed foreign; they were poor and unskilled; and they were arriving in overwhelming numbers. The Irish are perhaps the only people in our history with the distinction of having a political party, the Know-Nothings, formed against them. Their religion was later also the target of the American Protective Association and, in this century, the Ku Klux Klan.

The Irish found many doors closed to them, both socially and economically. Advertisements for jobs specified: "No Irish need apply." But there was manual labor to be done, and the Irish were ready to do it. They went to work as longshoremen, as ditch-diggers or as construction workers. When their earnings were not enough to support their families, their wives and daughters obtained employment as servants.

Contractors usually met them at the dock. The Erie Canal, linking New York with the Great Lakes in 1825, and other canals in Massachusetts, New Jersey, Pennsylvania and Maryland were largely built by Irish labor. But the canals soon became obsolete, and the frenzied building of railroads followed. In the three decades from 1830 to 1860, a network of thirty thousand miles of rails was laid across the middle part of the country. Again Irish labor furnished the muscle. When railroad construction was pushed westward in the latter part of the century, the Irish again figured prominently, by now often as foremen and section bosses. They also provided, at the same time, a supply of cheap labor for the mills of Rhode Island and Massachusetts and the coal mines of Pennsylvania.

But as the years passed and new generations were born, things began to change. Gradually, rung by rung, the Irish climbed up

NOVA BRITANNIA.

OFFERING MOST,

Excellent fruites by Planting in VIRGINIA.

Exciting all such as be well affected to further the same.

LONDON
Printed for SAMVEL MACHAM, and are to be sold at
his Shop in Pauls Church-yard, at the
Signe of the Bul-head.
1 6 0 9.

1

The first Americans—members of scattered tribes—were native-born. All others were immigrants. Some came early, some later. After the centuries of exploration, when men came to discover and conquer but did not stay to settle, the first community in what is now the Continental United States was founded by the Spanish in St. Augustine, Florida, in 1565. Sir Walter Raleigh built a colony farther up the Atlantic coast in 1585 and called it Virginia; another colony at Roanoke was lost and its fate is still a mystery. In 1606, King James I of England granted charters for new settlements in Virginia. The illustration here is the title page of a leaflet printed in London in 1609 for the Council of Virginia to persuade Englishmen to emigrate. In the years to come many such leaflets, handbills and advertisements, steamship posters, and letters from colonists carried the good news of a land of freedom and opportunity.

2

Many of the first immigrants, like many of the most recent, came to America to escape oppression at home. Religious persecution led thousands to the New World—the Puritans to Massachusetts, Quakers to Pennsylvania and Delaware, French Huguenots to South Carolina. Above is a depiction from a contemporary document of the burning of religious books in Salzburg, part of the religious persecution that drove Lutherans to America. Some came to Georgia in 1732. Below, a contemporary drawing shows James Nailor, a Quaker, who, because of his religious belief, was whipped in 1656 by the hangman in London, his tongue bored through with a hot iron and his forehead branded. Such men came to America in search of freedom to worship God as their conscience directed.

James Nailor Quaker set 2 howers on the Pillory at Westminster whiped by the Hangman to the old Exchainge London, Som dayes after, Stood too howers more on the Pillory in at the Exchainge, and there had his Tongue Bored throug with a hot Iron, & Stigmatized in the Forehead with the Letter:B; Decemr 17 anno Doini 1656:

TO BE SOLD, on **board** the *George-Town* Galley, *Thomas Crofthwaite* Mafter, lying at *Frankland's* Wharff, fundry *Englifh SERVANTS*, Men and Women, well recommended, amongft whom are **Tradef-**men, Hufbandmen, *&c.* indented for *Four Years.*

Many of the first settlers did not come as free men. Thousands, unemployed and homeless, signed away their freedom for a few years in exchange for transportation, coming as indentured servants to work without wages. Redemptioners agreed to be sold in America for the sum of their passage. Above, an advertisement for "English servants, Men and Women, well recommended . . . indent[ur]ed for Four Years."

At right is the deck plan of an eighteenth-century British slave ship. The first African slaves were brought in 1619 to Virginia. All such traffic in human lives was outlawed by vote of Congress in 1807, although many slaves were brought in illegally thereafter. Not until the Emancipation Proclamation in 1863, the war between North and South, and the ratification of the Thirteenth Amendment in 1865 were the slaves finally free. It took another century for freedom to be transformed into the beginning of first-class citizenship.

7

In the first half of the nineteenth century, immigration soared. Between 1815 and 1860, five million came. The largest number sailed from Ireland, victimized by starvation and typhus that followed the potato famine of 1845–1849. Crops failed, too, in Germany and in Holland, and many thousands, driven from the land, emigrated to the United States. Desperate families sold their last possessions for transportation, and in many cases landowners provided funds, wishing to free themselves of responsibility for a pauper class. Conditions on the crowded ships were often brutal, and a high percentage died before they reached the land of new hope. Above is a contemporary illustration of Irish famine victims.

Driven by economic need and the defeat of democracy in the revolutions of 1830 and 1848, well over a million Germans came in the fifteen years before 1860. Many were students and intellectuals, among them the social reformer Carl Schurz. Political refugees came also from other lands. Bohemian nationalists joined the Germans. Poles fled after the failure of revolts against alien rule of their country. Hungarians, defeated in their struggle for freedom in 1848, sought a new life in America. Above is a contemporary illustration of fighting between the Prussian army and revolutionists at the barricades in Frankfurt.

"Native Americans," native in the sense that their families had arrived in America earlier than some others, provoked anti-foreign riots in the 1840's. Men were killed and Catholic churches burned by mobs. About 1850 "Native Americans" formed a secret society, the Order of the Star-Spangled Banner. Members were instructed to answer "I know nothing" when questioned about their activities and consequently were labeled "Know-Nothings." For a few years they were a political power, electing governors in a number of states. Differences among them over the slavery issue led to a rapid decline of their influence in the years just before the Civil War. Above is a lithograph of a Philadelphia mob, in tall beaver hats, attacking the state militia in an anti-Catholic riot.

From 1870 to the end of the century, more than eleven million persons came to America, an increasing number from southern and eastern Europe and the Near East. The Burlingame Treaty with China in 1868 permitted Chinese immigration, and several thousand came, most to settle in California. But as American workers began to fear for their jobs, and as the depression of 1873 caused widespread unemployment, mobs fought the Chinese, killing some and burning the homes of others. The scene on the opposite page shows an anti-Chinese riot in Denver. The Chinese Exclusion Act of 1882 prohibited the immigration of Chinese laborers and denied American citizenship to native Chinese, a discriminatory act that remained in effect until World War II.

American immigrants gave their strength and skills to build a new country. Among the pioneers who moved West in the covered wagons to the open frontier were thousands of men and women who had just arrived in America. Inexpensive land lured many farmers to the Midwest. The Western railroads, built with the help of subsidies and land grants from the government, sold the land to get funds to build the roads. They sent agents to Europe to hunt for prospective immigrants, and advertised widely overseas. Upper right, an advertisement of the Illinois Central describing farms of $8 to $12 an acre available with long credit in Illinois, "the Garden State of America." Lower right, a pioneer's sod home on the Nebraska prairie, South Loup, Custer County, 1892.

Wheat — Corn — Cotton — Fruits & Vegetables

EQUAL TO ANY IN THE WORLD!!!

MAY BE PROCURED

At FROM $8 to $12 PER ACRE.

Near Markets, Schools, Railroads, Churches, and all the blessings of Civilization.
,200,000 Acres, in Farms of 40, 80, 120, 160 Acres and upwards, in
ILLINOIS, the Garden State of America.

Immigrants helped America make the transition to an industrial society. Chinese and Irish railroad gangs, recruited to meet the urgent labor demands, laid tracks that brought the East and West together in 1869, the Chinese from the West on the Central Pacific, the Irish from the East on the Union Pacific. Here, a photograph of the construction of the St. Paul, Minneapolis and Manitoba Railroad in 1887.

14

Immigrants—many from Scandinavia—were recruited for the lumber crews that felled timber in the Great Northwest. Here a crew poses for its portrait in 1906.

15

16 The great coal and steel industries owed much to the immigrant groups, among them the Welsh and Poles who came to Pennsylvania and Ohio in the nineteenth century. Here, a scene in an anthracite mine.

The New Colossus.

Not like the brazen giant of Greek fame,
With conquering limbs astride from land to land;
Here at our sea-washed, sunset-gates shall stand
A mighty woman with a torch, whose flame
Is the imprisoned lightning, and her name
Mother of Exiles. From her beacon-hand
Glows world-wide welcome, her mild eyes command
The air-bridged harbor that twin-cities frame.

"Keep, ancient lands, your storied pomp!" cries she
With silent lips. "Give me your tired, your poor,
Your huddled masses yearning to breathe free,
The wretched refuse of your teeming shore,
Send these, the homeless, tempest-tost to me,
I lift my lamp beside the golden door!"

Emma Lazarus.

November 2nd 1883.

The Statue of Liberty in New York Harbor has symbolized freedom for generations of immigrants. Mounted on its pedestal is a tablet reproducing a poem, "The New Colossus." It was written in 1883 by Emma Lazarus, who was born in New York of Jewish parentage and who was deeply concerned with the plight of Jews driven from Russia to the United States. The original manuscript of her famous poem is reproduced above.

Future Americans crowded every available steamship. Here and on the opposite page are typical scenes on the decks of Atlantic liners in the first years of the twentieth century.

19

An Italian immigrant family stands on the deck of a ferry boat plying between Ellis Island, first stop for European immigrants, and New York City.
Between 1820 and 1963, more than five million Italians came to America.

21

An Italian family with their bundled belongings, waiting for instructions.
Many such families took jobs in heavy industry or on the railroad. Others
settled in the urban centers of the East.

22

Persons of all races, all nations, and all conditions of life sought refuge in
America.

23

24 At Ellis Island, immigrants in the early 1900's anxiously wait to learn whether they will be permitted to enter the Promised Land of America.

25

Immigrants at Ellis Island answered questions, submitted to physical and psychological examinations, and then (if admitted) were ready to be transported to their destinations. Some unfortunate ones were rejected. Steamship companies, by an act of Congress in 1891, were compelled to carry back to Europe all passengers rejected by United States inspectors. Above, women immigrants at a medical examination on Ellis Island around 1910. On the opposite page, above, an inspector gives an intelligence test; below, immigrants are handed tags listing assignments to railroad cars for transportation to their next destination.

26

27

28   *German*   29   *Armenian*

The strong, dynamic faces of new Americans from eight countries, typical

30   *Danish*   31   *Czech*

32   *Laplander*   **33**   *Polish*

of those who came from many lands and from all of the inhabited continents:

34   *Chinese*   **35**   *Albanian*

Many immigrants got no farther than their first stop, New York City. Thousands settled in the Lower East Side, living in crowded tenements, as here (above) at Hester and Clinton streets.

(Opposite page) Sweatshops were organized in tenement homes and lofts during the first years of the twentieth century. Even children were pressed into work as families struggled to survive.

39 The hooded legions of the Ku Klux Klan brought terror to American Negroes, Catholics, Jews, and to almost all immigrant groups. The night riders used whips and guns and the lynching rope to spread their gospel of hate. Here, a photograph of a Klan rally reproduced from a Klan magazine of the 1920's.

The Pledge of Allegiance to the American flag at a citizenship class in 1940.

41

Symbol of the Nazi cancer that was to consume much of Europe is the above photograph of book burning by Nazi students in 1933. Thousands of books were destroyed by young fanatics. With the rise of Hitler and virulent anti-Semitism in the 1930's, millions of Jews tried desperately to escape from Germany and Nazi-occupied countries. Many nations of Europe, as well as the United States, were reluctant to admit the despairing multitudes. Before the end, six million Jews had died in concentration camps and gas chambers. But some escaped from the Nazis. Below, Albert Einstein, one of the greatest scientists in history, takes the Oath of Allegiance to the United States, with his daughter, Margot (right), in Trenton, New Jersey.

42

"What Happened To The One We Used To Have?"

From *The Herblock Book* (Beacon Press, 1952)

Restrictive immigration policy, stimulated in the 1920's by fear of competition from foreign labor and by the onset of isolationism, continued down to and through World War II. While thousands waited in despair for the Golden Door to open, Americans debated. Here, an eloquent 1946 cartoon by Herblock denouncing the lack of compassion of Americans who had forgotten their history and their own origins.

44

Refugees from Europe, victims of Nazi persecution and of war, came to America when the gates were opened. In 1948 Congress passed the Displaced Persons Act to admit more than 400,000. Above, the arrival of DP's in the early 1950's; opposite page, a reunion on the docks of New York, around 1947.

46

Political persecution was not ended by the destruction of Nazism or by the victory of World War II. Hundreds of thousands were made homeless in the 1950's by Communist oppression behind the Iron Curtain. In 1953 Congress passed the Refugee Relief Act to admit around 200,000 refugees, and this act made it possible for approximately 30,000 freedom fighters who escaped from Hungary after the 1956 anti-Soviet revolution to be admitted to the United States. Here a family crosses the icy marshland at Andau, Austria, in November, 1956, on their flight to freedom. During those weeks more than a thousand a day escaped through Andau.

the economic and social ladder. Some settled on farms, especially along the canals they had dug. But it was in the cities that they found their principal outlet, in areas in which they could demonstrate their abilities of self-expression, of administration and organization. They gravitated first into law and from that into politics and government. Having experienced for themselves the handicaps of illiteracy, they were determined that their children would have the advantages of education. To that end, they not only started parochial schools, but founded such institutions of higher learning as Notre Dame, Fordham, Holy Cross, Villanova, St. Louis University, Catholic University and Georgetown. They became teachers, writers, journalists, labor organizers, orators and priests. As an expanding society offered more opportunities, they swelled not only the civil service rosters, but the ranks of clerical and administrative workers in industry.

The Irish eased the way for other immigrant groups and speeded their assimilation in several ways. They firmly established the Catholic Church, originally French on this continent, as an English-speaking institution. The schools they founded offered educational opportunities to children of later immigrants of other tongues. The Irish had their own press, their own fraternal orders and their own charitable organizations.

Irish labor leaders fought for the rights of other groups as well as their own. Workers of Irish descent helped organize the Knights of Labor, the first big national union, which was a forerunner of the American Federation of Labor.

THE GERMANS

Between 1830 and 1930, the period of the greatest migration from Europe to the United States, Germany sent six million people to the United States—more than any other nation. Their migrations, increasing in numbers after 1850, overlapped the Irish, whose immigration declined.

The Germans were unique among immigrant groups in their wide dispersal, both geographically and occupationally. This was due, at least in part, to the fact that most of them came with some

resources, and were not forced to cluster along the Eastern seaboard. Attracted to the United States by cheap public and
railroad lands, and later by free homesteads, the German farmer
helped to farm the New West and to cultivate the Mississippi
Valley. German artisans, much sought after because of their
skills, became an important factor in industrial expansion.

Almost every state in the Union profited from their intellectual
and material contributions. Hard-working and knowledgeable
about agricultural methods, the Germans became propagators of
scientific farming, crop rotation, soil conservation. They share
with the Scandinavians the credit for turning millions of acres
of wilderness into productive farm land.

The urban settlers lent a distinctive German flavor to many of
our cities. Cincinnati, then known as "Queen City" of the West,
Baltimore, St. Louis, Minneapolis and Milwaukee, all had substantial German populations. Milwaukee has perhaps retained
its distinctive German character longer than any of the others.

In these urban centers Germans entered the fields of education,
science, engineering and the arts. German immigrants founded
and developed industrial enterprises in the fields of lumbering,
food-processing, brewing, steel-making, electrical engineering,
piano-making, railroading and printing.

A small but significant part of the German immigration consisted of political refugees. Reaction in Germany against the
reform ideas of the French Revolution had caused heavy suppression of liberal thought. There was strict censorship of the
press, of public meetings and of the schools and universities.
Nevertheless, a liberal movement had emerged, nurtured in the
universities by young intellectuals. This movement led to unsuccessful revolutions in 1830 and 1848. The United States
welcomed a large number of veterans of 1848—men of education,
substance and social standing, like Carl Schurz, the statesman
and reformer, and General Franz Sigel. In addition, some of the
German religious groups established utopian communities in parts
of Pennsylvania, Ohio, Indiana, Texas and Oregon.

German immigration reflected all the chaotic conditions of
Central Europe after Napoleon: the population growth, the wide-

spread hunger, the religious dissension and oppression. The Germans included Lutherans, Jews and Catholics, as well as freethinkers. Their talents, training and background greatly enriched the burgeoning nation.

To the influence of the German immigrants in particular— although all minority groups contributed—we owe the mellowing of the austere Puritan imprint on our daily lives. The Puritans observed the Sabbath as a day of silence and solemnity. The Germans clung to their concept of the "Continental Sunday" as a day, not only of churchgoing, but also of relaxation, of picnics, of visiting, of quiet drinking in beer gardens while listening to the music of a band.

The Christmas ritual of religious services combined with exchanging gifts around the Christmas tree is of German origin. So, too, is the celebration of the New Year.

The fact that today almost every large American city has its symphony orchestra can be traced to the influence of the German migration. Leopold Damrosch and his son, Walter, helped build the famous New York Philharmonic. Originally composed mainly of German immigrant musicians and called the Germania Orchestra, it became the seed bed of similar organizations all over the country. This tradition was carried to the Midwest by Frederick Stock and to Boston by Carl Zerrahn. Others spread this form of cultural expression to additional urban centers throughout the land.

Community singing and glee clubs owe much to the German immigrant, who remembered his singing societies. The first *Männerchor* was founded in Philadelphia in 1835; the first *Liederkranz* was organized in Baltimore in 1836. Their counterparts have been a feature of the German-American community everywhere.

The ideas of German immigrants helped to shape our educational system. They introduced the kindergarten, or "children's play school." They also promoted the concept of the state-endowed university, patterned after the German university. The University of Michigan, founded in 1837, was the first such school to add to the philosophy of general liberal arts educa-

tion an emphasis upon vocational training. The colonial concept
of a university as a place to prepare gentlemen for a life of
leisured culture was modified to include training in specialized
skills.

The program of physical education in the schools had its
roots in the *Turnverein,* or German gymnastic society. It was
adopted and introduced to the American public by the YMCA.

German immigrant influence has been pervasive, in our
language, in our mores, in our customs and in our basic philosophy. Even the hamburger, the frankfurter and the delicatessen,
that omnipresent neighborhood institution, came to us via the
German immigrants.

Although they were mostly Democrats prior to 1850, the
Germans broke party lines in the decade before the Civil War
and played a prominent part in the formation of the Republican
party. They were most united on two issues. They opposed the
Blue Laws, and they vigorously fought the extension of slavery
into new territories. Indeed, the first protest against Negro
slavery came from Germantown settlers, led by Franz Pastorius,
in 1688.

During the Civil War they fought on both sides. Following the
Civil War, Germans infused the faltering American labor movement with new strength by organizing craft unions for printers,
watchmakers, carpenters, ironworkers, locksmiths, butchers and
bakers.

Adjusting with relative ease, they did not feel the sting of
ethnic discrimination until the outbreak of the First World War,
when they became targets of wartime hysteria. This hysteria
even caused overardent "patriots" to call sauerkraut "Liberty
cabbage" and hamburger "Salisbury steak." Nonetheless, when
the United States entered the war in 1917, men of German
ancestry entered the armed forces of the United States and
served with distinction.

As the Second World War drew near, Americans of German
descent faced another test. Only a few joined the pro-Nazi
German-American Bund, and many of those left as soon as they
discovered its real nature. More "older Americans" than those of

German descent could be counted in the ranks of America-Firsters. Again, after the U.S. was attacked, descendants of German immigrants fought with valor in our armed services.

THE SCANDINAVIANS

Scandinavian immigrants left their homelands for economic rather than political or religious reasons. In America they found a political and social climate wholly compatible with their prior experience. Democratic institutions and a homogeneous society were already developing in Scandinavia, in an atmosphere of comparative tranquillity.

The seemingly limitless availability of farm land in America was an attractive prospect to land-hungry people.

The tide of Scandinavian immigration overlapped the tide of German immigration just as the Germans overlapped the Irish. The Swedes came first. They started coming about 1840, reaching their crest after 1860. Between 1840 and 1930, about 1.3 million Swedes came to the United States. In the 1880's migrations of other Scandinavians—Danes, Finns, Icelanders and principally the Norwegians—also reached their peak.

Following the Erie Canal and the Great Lakes, the Swedes pushed westward until they found a familiar landscape in the prairie states of the upper Mississippi Valley. There they settled.

The first colony of these Swedes settled at a place they named Pine Lakes (now New Upsala), in Wisconsin, in 1841. Later colonists showed a preference for a broad belt of land extending westward from Michigan, through Illinois, Wisconsin, Minnesota, Nebraska, Iowa and Kansas.

Other Scandinavian migrations followed more or less the same geographical pattern, except for the Norwegians. Although not so large numerically as other immigrant groups, Norwegian immigration in proportion to their population at home was second only to the Irish. Some of the Norwegians drove far west to the Dakotas, Oregon and Washington. Norwegian immigration to the United States is estimated at 840,000; Danes at 350,000. Most Scandinavians settled in rural areas, except for the Finns, some of whom went to work in the copper mines of Michigan or the iron mines of Minnesota.

Physically hardy, conditioned by the rigors of life at home to withstand the hardships of the frontier, the Scandinavians made ideal pioneers. Ole Rölvaag, the Norwegian-American novelist, movingly chronicled their struggles in *Giants in the Earth*.

Often they started their homesteading in sod huts, some of which were no more than holes in a hillside shored up with logs, with greased-paper windows. They looked forward to the day they could live in a log cabin or in a house. Then began the struggle with the unrelenting forces of nature: hailstorms, droughts, blizzards, plagues of grasshoppers and locusts. But they endured.

America was an expanding continent in urgent need of housing. It was the Swedes, familiar with the ax and the saw—called "the Swedish fiddle"—who went into the forests across the Northern United States, felled the logs, slid them into the streams and sent them on their way to the mills, where they were cut into boards to provide shelter for millions of other immigrants. Norwegians and Finns were also among the loggers. On the West Coast the Norwegians tended to become fishermen.

The Swedes did many other things too. In the long nights of the Swedish winter, they had learned to fashion things with their hands and had become skilled craftsmen and artisans. The "do-it-yourself" hobbyist of today is an avocational descendant of the Swedes. Manual training in our own public school system is derived from a basic course in the Swedish schools.

The Scandinavians were avid supporters of the public school system. And they contributed to the school system and to education generally in a variety of ways. The home economics courses of our public schools were introduced by Scandinavians. They also helped launch adult education programs. The 4-H Clubs, now an international as well as a national institution, were originated at a farm school in Minnesota by Americans of Scandinavian descent. A number of colleges today stand as monuments to the early efforts of Norwegians and Swedes to make higher learning available. Among these are Augustana College in Illinois, Gustavus Adolphus in Minnesota, Bethany College in Kansas and Luther College in Nebraska. All were founded by Swedish immigrants. Luther College in Iowa and St. Olaf College in Minnesota were founded by the Norwegians. They have added to our cultural life with their choral groups and singing societies.

With their background, it was inevitable that the Swedes would develop many engineers, scientists and inventors. One of the most famous was John Ericsson, who not only designed the *Monitor*, one of the first armor-clad ships, but also perfected the screw propeller.

The Danes, who had an intimate knowledge of animal husbandry, laid the foundations of our dairy industry and early creamery cooperatives. Together with the Germans and the Swiss, they developed cheese-making into an American industry.

Since the Danes were primarily agriculturists, it is curious that the one who made the most distinctive individual contribution was a city boy, Jacob Riis. As a crusading journalist and documentary photographer, he exposed the conditions under which other immigrants lived and worked in New York, and was instrumental in bringing about major social reforms.

Politically, Scandinavians cannot be classified into a single mold. At times they have been conservative. At times they have provided support for such liberal movements as the Farmer-Labor party, Senator Robert M. La Follette's Progressive party and the Non-Partisan League. Both major parties have benefited from Scandinavian political thought, and both major parties have had Scandinavians in both state and federal office.

OTHER IMMIGRANT GROUPS

Toward the end of the nineteenth century, emigration to America underwent a significant change. Large numbers of Italians, Russians, Poles, Czechs, Hungarians, Rumanians, Bulgarians, Austrians and Greeks began to arrive. Their coming created new problems and gave rise to new tensions.

For these people the language barrier was even greater than
it had been for earlier groups, and the gap between the world
they had left behind and the one to which they came was
wider. For the most part, these were people of the land and, for
the most part, too, they were forced to settle in the cities when
they reached America. Most large cities had well-defined "Little
Italys" or "Little Polands" by 1910. In the 1960 census, New
York City had more people of Italian birth or parentage than did
Rome.

The history of cities shows that when conditions become over-
crowded, when people are poor and when living conditions are
bad, tensions run high. This is a situation that feeds on itself;
poverty and crime in one group breed fear and hostility in
others. This, in turn, impedes the acceptance and progress of
the first group, thus prolonging its depressed condition. This
was the dismal situation that faced many of the Southern and
Eastern European immigrants just as it had faced some of
the earlier waves of immigrants. One New York newspaper had
these intemperate words for the newly arrived Italians: "The
flood gates are open. The bars are down. The sally-ports are un-
guarded. The dam is washed away. The sewer is choked . . .
the scum of immigration is viscerating upon our shores. The
horde of $9.60 steerage slime is being siphoned upon us from
Continental mud tanks."

Italy has contributed more immigrants to the United States
than any country except Germany. Over five million Italians
came to this country between 1820 and 1963. Large-scale immigration began in 1880, and almost four million Italian immigrants
arrived in the present century.

The first Italians were farmers and artisans from northern
Italy. Some planted vineyards in Vineland, New Jersey, in the
Finger Lakes region of New York State and in California, where
they inaugurated our domestic wine industry. Others settled on
the periphery of cities, where they started truck gardens.

But most Italians were peasants from the south. They came
because of neither religious persecution nor political repression,
but simply in search of a brighter future. Population in Italy was

straining the limits of the country's resources and more and more people had to eke out a living from small plots of land, held in many instances by oppressive landlords.

In many ways the experience of the later Italian immigrants parallels the story of the Irish. Mostly farmers, their lack of financial resources kept them from reaching the rural areas of the United States. Instead, they crowded into cities along the Eastern seaboard, often segregating themselves by province, even by village, in a density as high as four thousand to the city block.

Untrained in special skills and unfamiliar with the language, they had to rely on unskilled labor jobs to earn a living. Italians thus filled the gap left by earlier immigrant groups who had now moved up the economic ladder. As bricklayers, masons, stonecutters, ditchdiggers and hod carriers, they helped build our cities, subways and skyscrapers. They worked on the railroads and the dams, went into the coal mines, iron mines and factories. Some found a place in urban life as small storekeepers, peddlers, shoemakers, barbers and tailors. Wages were small and families were large. In the old country everyone worked. Here everyone worked too. Wives went into the needle trades. Boys picked up what pennies they could as news vendors, bootblacks and errand-runners. Through these difficult years of poverty, toil and bewilderment, the Italians were bolstered by their adherence to the church, the strength of their family ties, Italian-language newspapers and their fraternal orders. But they overcame obstacles of prejudice and misunderstanding quickly, and they have found places of importance in almost every phase of American life. Citizens of Italian descent are among our leading bankers, contractors, food importers, educators, labor leaders and government officials. Italians have made special contributions to the emergence of American culture, enriching our music, art and architecture.

An Italian, Filippo Traetta (Philip Trajetta), founded the American Conservatory in Boston in 1800, and another in Philadelphia shortly thereafter. Another Italian, Lorenzo da Ponte, brought the first Italian opera troupe to New York in 1832, where it developed into a permanent institution. Italians have founded and supported the opera as an institution in New York, Chicago, San Francisco and other large cities, providing from their ranks many impresarios and singers. Italian-born music teachers and bandmasters are numerous. Arturo Toscanini, for many years leader of the New York Philharmonic, and our most distinguished conductor of recent years, was Italian-born.

Italians have also been among our most prominent sculptors, architects and artists. A West Indian and a Frenchman designed our nation's Capitol. An Italian beautified it. Constantino Brumidi painted the historical frieze in the rotunda of the Capitol building. Other Italian painters and sculptors depicted our history in paintings, murals, friezes and statues. Historical monuments and statues up and down the country have been wrought by Italian-American sculptors. On a humbler scale, the taste and skill of Italian-American landscape gardeners and architects have placed our homes and communities in beautiful settings.

About the time the Italians began coming, other great tides of immigration from the countries of Eastern and Southeastern Europe also began arriving in the United States. In the years between 1820 and 1963 these areas, Italy included, sent over fifteen million immigrants to our shores.

They came for all manner of reasons: political upheavals, religious persecution, hopes for economic betterment. They comprised a wide ethnic variety, from Lithuanians and Latvians on the Baltic to Greeks, Turks and Armenians on the eastern Mediterranean. They brought with them a bewildering variety of language, dress, custom, ideology and religious belief. To many Americans already here who had grown accustomed to a common way of life, they presented a dismaying bedlam, difficult to understand and more difficult to respond to. Indeed, because of the many changes in national boundaries and prior migrations of races within that area of Europe, there is no way of accurately reporting on them statistically.

The largest number from any of these countries of Eastern Europe were Poles, who for 125 years had been under the domination of Russia, Germany and Austria-Hungary. Some followed the pattern of the Germans and Scandinavians, settling on individual farms or forming small rural communities which still bear Polish place names. But most gravitated to the cities. Four-fifths were Roman Catholic. Longer than most immigrant groups they kept their language, their customs and their dances. At first, like other immigrants, they lived under substandard conditions. Gradually they, too, improved their status. They aspired to own their own homes and their own plots of land. In Hamtramck, Michigan, an almost wholly Polish community, three-quarters of the residents own their own homes.

By 1963, almost 130,000 Czechs had migrated to this country. They tended to gravitate to the farming communities. It is one of these homesteads that is portrayed by novelist Willa Cather in *My Antonia*. They also formed enclaves in cities, principally in Chicago, Cleveland and New York.

A potent force in the development of Czech life in this country has been the *Sokol*, a traditional cultural, social and gymnastic society. These societies stressed high standards of physical fitness and an interest in singing, music and literature.

The immigrants from Old Russia are estimated at almost three and a half million. Most of this wave of immigration went into the mines and factories. However, there were also many Russian intellectuals, scientists, scholars, musicians, writers and artists, who came here usually during periods of political oppression.

Most students of the history of immigration to America make special mention of the Jews. Although they appeared as part of several of the waves of immigration, they warrant separate discussion because of their religion, culture and historical background.

In colonial times most Jews in America were of Spanish-Portuguese origin. Throughout the nineteenth century most came from Germany. Beginning at the end of the nineteenth century they began to come in large numbers from Russia, Poland, Austria-Hungary, Rumania and, in smaller numbers, from almost every European nation. The American Jewish population today numbers approximately six million.

The Jews who came during the early nineteenth century were often peddlers, wandering throughout the land with their packs and their carts or settling down to open small stores. They prospered in this era of opportunity and expansion, for from these humble beginnings have grown many of our large department stores and mercantile establishments.

The exodus from Germany after 1848 brought Jewish intellectuals, philosophers, educators, political leaders and social reformers. These shared much the same experiences as the other immigrants. "Like the Scandinavian Lutherans and the Irish Catholics," says Oscar Handlin, "they appeared merely to maintain their distinctive heritage while sharing the rights and obligations of other Americans within a free society."

At the turn of the century the Jews fleeing persecution in Russia came in such numbers that they could not be so readily absorbed into the mainstream of life as the earlier comers. They clustered in Jewish communities within the large cities, like New York.

Like the Irish and the Italians before them, they had to work at whatever they could find. Most found an outlet for their skills in the needle trades, as garment workers, hatmakers and furriers. Often they worked in sweatshops. In an effort to improve working conditions (which involved child labor and other forms of exploitation), they joined with other immigrant workers to form, in 1900, the International Ladies' Garment Workers Union. In time, they developed the clothing industry as we know it today, centered in New York but reaching into every small town and rural area. The experience and tradition of these pioneers produced many effective leaders in the labor movement, such as Morris Hillquit, Sidney Hillman, Jacob Potofsky and David Dubinsky.

Jewish immigrants have also made immense contributions to thought: as scholars, as educators, as scientists, as judges and lawyers, as journalists, as literary figures. Refugee scientists such as Albert Einstein and Edward Teller brought great scientific knowledge to this country.

Immigration from the Orient in the latter part of the nineteenth century was confined chiefly to California and the West Coast. Our behavior toward these groups of newcomers represented a shameful episode in our relationships to those seeking the hospitality of our shores. They were often mobbed and stoned by native Americans. The Chinese suffered and were barred from our shores as far back as the Chinese Exclusion Act of 1882. After the Japanese attack on Pearl Harbor many Japanese-Americans were victimized by prejudice and unreasoning discrimination. They were arbitrarily shipped to relocation camps. It took the extraordinary battlefield accomplishments of the nisei, Americans of Japanese descent, fighting in the U.S. Army in Europe, to help restore our perspective. While our attitude toward these citizens has been greatly improved over the years, many inequities in the law regarding Oriental immigration must still be redressed.

Today many of our newcomers are from Mexico and Puerto Rico. We sometimes forget that Puerto Ricans are U.S. citizens by birth and therefore cannot be considered immigrants. Nonetheless, they often receive the same discriminatory treatment and opprobrium that were faced by other waves of newcomers. The same things are said today of Puerto Ricans and Mexicans that were once said of Irish, Italians, Germans and Jews: "They'll never adjust; they can't learn the language; they won't be absorbed."

Perhaps our brightest hope for the future lies in the lessons of the past. The people who have come to this country have made America, in the words of one perceptive writer, "a heterogeneous race but a homogeneous nation."

In sum, then, we can see that as each new wave of immigration has reached America it has been faced with problems, not only the problems that come with making new homes and learning new jobs, but, more important, the problems of getting along with people of different backgrounds and habits.

Each new group was met by the groups already in America, and adjustment was often difficult and painful. The early English settlers had to find ways to get along with the Indians; the Irish who followed were met by these "Yankees"; German immigrants faced both Yankee and Irish; and so it has gone down to the latest group of Hungarian refugees. Somehow, the difficult adjustments are made and people get down to the tasks of earning a living, raising a family, living with their new neighbors and, in the process, building a nation.

CHAPTER 5

The Immigrant Contribution

Oscar Handlin has said, "Once I thought to write a history of the immigrants in America. Then I discovered that the immigrants *were* American history." In the same sense, we cannot really speak of a particular "immigrant contribution" to America because all Americans have been immigrants or the descendants of immigrants; even the Indians, as mentioned before, migrated to the American continent. We can only speak of people whose roots in America are older or newer. Yet each wave of immigration left its own imprint on American society; each made its distinctive "contribution" to the building of the nation and the evolution of American life. Indeed, if, as some of the older immigrants like to do, we were to restrict the definition of immigrants to the 42 million people who came to the United States *after* the Declaration of Independence, we would have to conclude that our history and our society would have been vastly different if they all had stayed at home.

As we have seen, people migrated to the United States for a variety of reasons. But nearly all shared two great hopes: the hope for personal freedom and the hope for economic opportunity. In consequence, the impact of immigration has been broadly to confirm the impulses in American life demanding more political liberty and more economic growth.

So, of the fifty-six signers of the Declaration of Independence, eighteen were of non-English stock and eight were first-generation immigrants. Two immigrants—the West Indian Alexander Hamilton, who was Washington's Secretary of the Treasury, and the Swiss Albert Gallatin, who held the same office under Jefferson—established the financial policies of the young republic. A German farmer wrote home from Missouri in 1834,

> If you wish to see our whole family living in . . . a country where freedom of speech obtains, where no spies are eavesdropping, where no simpletons criticize your every word and seek to detect therein a venom that might endanger the life of the state, the church and the home, in short, if you wish to be really happy and independent, then come here.

Every ethnic minority, in seeking its own freedom, helped strengthen the fabric of liberty in American life.

Similarly, every aspect of the American economy has profited from the contributions of immigrants. We all know, of course, about the spectacular immigrant successes: the men who came from foreign lands, sought their fortunes in the United States and made striking contributions, industrial and scientific, not only to their chosen country but to the entire world. In 1953 the President's Commission on Immigration and Naturalization mentioned the following:

Industrialists: Andrew Carnegie (Scot), in the steel industry; John Jacob Astor (German), in the fur trade; Michael Cudahy (Irish), of the meat-packing industry; the Du Ponts (French), of the munitions and chemical industry; Charles L. Fleischmann (Hungarian), of the yeast business; David Sarnoff (Russian), of the radio industry; and William S. Knudsen (Danish), of the automobile industry.

Scientists and inventors: Among those whose genius has benefited the United States are Albert Einstein (German), in physics; Michael Pupin (Serbian), in electricity; Enrico Fermi (Italian), in atomic research; John Ericsson (Swedish), who invented the ironclad ship and the screw propeller; Giuseppe Bellanca (Italian) and Igor Sikorsky (Russian), who made outstanding contributions to airplane development; John A. Udden (Swedish), who was responsible for opening the Texas oil fields; Lucas P. Kyrides (Greek), industrial chemistry; David Thomas (Welsh), who invented the hot blast furnace; Alexander Graham Bell (Scot), who

invented the telephone; Conrad Hubert (Russian), who invented
the flashlight; and Ottmar Mergenthaler (German), who invented
the linotype machine.

But the anonymous immigrant played his indispensable role
too. Between 1880 and 1920 America became the industrial and
agricultural giant of the world as well as the world's leading
creditor nation. This could not have been done without the hard
labor, the technical skills and the entrepreneurial ability of the
23.5 million people who came to America in this period.

Significant as the immigrant role was in politics and in the
economy, the immigrant contribution to the professions and the
arts was perhaps even greater. Charles O. Paullin's analysis of the
Dictionary of American Biography shows that, of the eighteenth-
and nineteenth-century figures, 20 percent of the businessmen,
20 percent of the scholars and scientists, 23 percent of the painters, 24 percent of the engineers, 28 percent of the architects, 29
percent of the clergymen, 46 percent of the musicians and 61 percent of the actors were of foreign birth—a remarkable measure of
the impact of immigration on American culture. And not only
have many American writers and artists themselves been immigrants or the children of immigrants, but immigration has provided American literature with one of its major themes.

Perhaps the most pervasive influence of immigration is to be
found in the innumerable details of life and the customs and
habits brought by millions of people who never became famous.
This impact was felt from the bottom up, and these contributions
to American institutions may be the ones which most intimately
affect the lives of all Americans.

In the area of religion, all the major American faiths were
brought to this country from abroad. The multiplicity of sects
established the American tradition of religious pluralism and
assured to all the freedom of worship and separation of church
and state pledged in the Bill of Rights.

So, too, in the very way we speak, immigration has altered
American life. In greatly enriching the American vocabulary, it
has been a major force in establishing "the American language,"
which, as H. L. Mencken demonstrated thirty years ago, had
diverged materially from the mother tongue as spoken in Britain.

Even the American dinner table has felt the impact. One writer
has suggested that "typical American menus" might include some
of the following dishes: "Irish stew, chop suey, goulash, chile con
carne, ravioli, knackwurst mit sauerkraut, Yorkshire pudding,
Welsh rarebit, borsch, gefilte fish, Spanish omelet, caviar, mayon-
naise, antipasto, baumkuchen, English muffins, Gruyère cheese,
Danish pastry, Canadian bacon, hot tamales, wiener schnitzel,
petits fours, spumone, bouillabaisse, maté, scones, Turkish coffee,
minestrone, filet mignon."

Immigration plainly was not always a happy experience. It
was hard on the newcomers, and hard as well on the communities
to which they came. When poor, ill-educated and frightened
people disembarked in a strange land, they often fell prey to
native racketeers, unscrupulous businessmen and cynical politi-
cians. Boss Tweed said, characteristically, in defense of his own
depredations in New York in the 1870's, "This population is too
hopelessly split into races and factions to govern it under universal
suffrage, except by bribery of patronage, or corruption."

But the very problems of adjustment and assimilation presented a challenge to the American idea—a challenge which subjected that idea to stern testing and eventually brought out the
best qualities in American society. Thus the public school became
a powerful means of preparing the newcomers for American
life. The ideal of the "melting pot" symbolized the process of
blending many strains into a single nationality, and we have come
to realize in modern times that the "melting pot" need not mean
the end of particular ethnic identities or traditions. Only in the
case of the Negro has the melting pot failed to bring a minority
into the full stream of American life. Today we are belatedly,
but resolutely, engaged in ending this condition of national
exclusion and shame and abolishing forever the concept of
second-class citizenship in the United States.

Sociologists call the process of the melting pot "social mobility."
One of America's characteristics has always been the lack of a
rigid class structure. It has traditionally been possible for people
to move up the social and economic scale. Even if one did not
succeed in moving up oneself, there was always the hope that
one's children would. Immigration is by definition a gesture of

faith in social mobility. It is the expression in action of a positive belief in the possibility of a better life. It has thus contributed greatly to developing the spirit of personal betterment in American society and to strengthening the national confidence in change and the future. Such confidence, when widely shared, sets the national tone. The opportunities that America offered made the dream real, at least for a good many; but the dream itself was in large part the product of millions of plain people beginning a new life in the conviction that life could indeed be better, and each new wave of immigration rekindled the dream.

This is the spirit which so impressed Alexis de Tocqueville, and which he called the spirit of equality. Equality in America has never meant literal equality of condition or capacity; there will always be inequalities in character and ability in any society. Equality has meant rather that, in the words of the Declaration of Independence, "all men are created equal . . . [and] are endowed by their Creator with certain unalienable rights"; it has meant that in a democratic society there should be no inequalities in opportunities or in freedoms. The American philosophy of equality has released the energy of the people, built the economy, subdued the continent, shaped and reshaped the structure of government, and animated the American attitude toward the world outside.

The *continuous* immigration of the nineteenth and early twentieth centuries was thus central to the whole American faith. It gave every old American a standard by which to judge how far he had come and every new American a realization of how far he might go. It reminded every American, old and new, that change is the essence of life, and that American society is a process, not a conclusion. The abundant resources of this land provided the foundation for a great nation. But only people could make the opportunity a reality. Immigration provided the human resources. More than that, it infused the nation with a commitment to far horizons and new frontiers, and thereby kept the pioneer spirit of American life, the spirit of equality and of hope, always alive and strong. "We are the heirs of all time," wrote Herman Melville, "and with all nations we divide our inheritance."

CHAPTER 6

Immigration Policy

◥

From the start, immigration policy has been a prominent subject of discussion in America. This is as it must be in a democracy, where every issue should be freely considered and debated.

Immigration, or rather the British policy of clamping down on immigration, was one of the factors behind the colonial desire for independence. Restrictive immigration policies constituted one of the charges against King George III expressed in the Declaration of Independence. And in the Constitutional Convention James Madison noted, "That part of America which has encouraged them [the immigrants] has advanced most rapidly in population, agriculture and the arts." So, too, Washington in his Thanksgiving Day Proclamation of 1795 asked all Americans "humbly and fervently to beseech the kind Author of these blessings . . . to render this country more and more a safe and propitious asylum for the unfortunate of other countries."

Yet there was the basic ambiguity which older Americans have often shown toward newcomers. In 1797 a member of Congress argued that, while a liberal immigration policy was fine when the country was new and unsettled, now that America had reached its maturity and was fully populated, immigration should stop—an argument which has been repeated at regular intervals throughout American history.

The fear of embroilment in the wars between Britain and France helped the cause of the restrictionists. In 1798 a Federalist Congress passed the Alien Act, authorizing the expulsion of foreigners "dangerous to the peace and safety of the United

States" and extending the residence requirement for naturalization from five to fourteen years. But the Alien Act, and its accompanying Sedition Act, went too far. Both acts were allowed to expire in 1801; the naturalization period went back to five years; and President Thomas Jefferson expressed the predominant American sentiment when he asked: "Shall we refuse to the unhappy fugitives from distress that hospitality which the savages of the wilderness extended to our fathers arriving in this land? Shall oppressed humanity find no asylum on this globe?"

But emotions of xenophobia—hatred of foreigners—and of nativism—the policy of keeping America "pure" (that is, of preferring old immigrants to new)—continued to thrive. The increase in the rate of immigration in the 1820's and 1830's set off new waves of hostility, directed especially against the Irish, who, as Catholics, were regarded as members of an alien conspiracy. Even Ralph Waldo Emerson could write to Thomas Carlyle about "the wild Irish element . . . led by Romanish Priests, who sympathize, of course, with despotism." Samuel F. B. Morse, the painter and inventor of the telegraph, wrote an anti-Catholic book entitled A Foreign Conspiracy Against the Liberties of the United States. Some alarmed Americans believed that every Catholic was a foreign agent dispatched by the Pope to subvert American society. In 1834 a mob burned down the Ursuline Convent school in Charlestown, Massachusetts. Though the leading citizens of Boston promptly denounced this act, anti-Catholic feeling persisted.

In the 1850's nativism became an open political movement. A secret patriotic society, the Order of the Star-Spangled Banner, founded about 1850, grew into the American party, whose members were pledged to vote only for native Americans, to demand a twenty-one-year naturalization period and to fight Roman Catholicism. When asked about their program, they were instructed to answer, "I know nothing about it," so people called them the Know-Nothings. Coming into existence at a time when the slavery issue was dissolving the older party allegiances, the Know-Nothings for a moment attracted considerable support.

They elected six state governors and seventy-five Congressmen in 1854 and got almost 25 percent of the vote for their candidate, former President Millard Fillmore, in 1856. But soon they, too, were split by the slavery issue, and the party vanished as quickly as it had appeared.

The legacy of the Know-Nothings lived beyond its life as an organization. The seeds of bigotry, fear and hatred bore fruit again in the years after the Civil War. The Ku Klux Klan launched a campaign of terrorism against the Negroes, and in the 1890's the American Protective Association tried to revive popular feeling against Catholics. Other nativists began to turn their attention to the Jews. In the meantime, agitators on the West Coast denounced the "yellow peril," and Congress in 1882 passed the first of a number of laws banning Oriental immigration. Yet, except for Oriental exclusion, Congress ignored the nativist clamor, and most Americans regarded nativism with abhorrence. When a Protestant clergyman supporting James G. Blaine in 1884 denounced the Democrats as the party of "rum, Romanism and rebellion," he provoked a reaction which may well have lost the election for Blaine, who himself had a mother of Irish Catholic descent.

The First World War led to another outbreak of nativism. A new group, adopting the program of the Know-Nothings and the name of the Ku Klux Klan, came into being, denouncing everything its members disliked—Negroes, Catholics, Jews, evolutionists, religious liberals, internationalists, pacifists—in the name of true Americanism and of "Nordic superiority." For a season, the new KKK prospered, claiming five million members, mostly in the South but also in Indiana, Ohio, Kansas and Maine. But, like the other nativist movements, the fall of the Klan was as dramatic as its rise. It died when a genuine crisis, the depression, turned people's attention away from the phony issue of racism to the real problems facing the nation. In later years, the Jew succeeded the Catholic as the chief target of nativist hysteria, and some Catholics, themselves so recently persecuted, now regrettably joined in the attack on the newer minorities.

America had no cause to be smug about the failure of these

movements to take deep root. Nativism failed, not because the seeds were not there to be cultivated, but because American society is too complex for an agitation so narrowly and viciously conceived to be politically successful. That the nativist movements found any response at all must cause us to look searchingly at ourselves. That the response was at times so great offers cause for alarm.

Still it remains a remarkable fact that, except for the Oriental Exclusion Act, there was no governmental response till after the First World War.

Not only were newcomers allowed to enter freely, but in some periods they were actively sought after.

Inevitably, though, this mass influx of people presented problems which the federal government was forced to recognize. In 1882, recognizing the need for a national immigration policy, Congress enacted the first general legislation on the subject. The most important aspect of this law was that, for the first time, the government undertook to exclude certain classes of undesirables, such as lunatics, convicts, idiots and persons likely to become public charges. In 1891 certain health standards were added as well as a provision excluding polygamists.

From time to time additional laws were added. The only deviation from the basic policy of free, nondiscriminatory immigration was the Oriental Exclusion Act.

Under a special treaty arrangement with China, nationals of that country had been guaranteed free and unrestricted immigration to the United States. At the peak of that immigration, in 1882, there were only forty thousand arrivals; even in 1890 there were but 107,000 Chinese in America. Most of them lived in California and had proved good and useful workers and citizens. Although they had originally been welcomed to America for their services in building railroads and reclaiming the land, the conviction began to grow that Chinese labor was undermining the standards of "American" labor. This became virtually an obsession with many people. In the early 1870's anti-Chinese agitation in California became organized and focused under the leadership of Denis Kearney, who was, ironically, an immigrant from Ireland. A campaign of organized violence against Chinese communities took form, and the hysteria led to political pressure too violent to be resisted. President Hayes vetoed an act of Congress restricting Chinese immigration, but he did force renegotiation of the Burlingame Treaty under which the government of China agreed to restrict emigration voluntarily. Not satisfied with this remedy, Congress then enacted and the President signed into law a series of measures shutting off almost completely immigration from China.

Shameful as these episodes were, they were, however, only an exception to the prevailing policy. A more serious warning of things to come was sounded in 1897 when Congress, for the first time, provided a literacy test for adult immigrants. President Cleveland vetoed the measure. Presidents Taft and Wilson vetoed similar bills on the ground that literacy was a test only of educational opportunity and not of a person's ability or his potential worth as a citizen. In 1917, with tension high because of the war, Congress overrode President Wilson's veto and the literacy test became law.

The twenty-year fight over the literacy test can now be seen as a significant turning point in immigration policy. Indeed, many saw it as such at that time. Finley Peter Dunne, creator of the immortal Mr. Dooley, devoted one of Mr. Dooley's dissertations in 1902 to the subject of the test and immigration. With magnificent irony the Irish bartender says, "As a pilgrim father that missed the first boat, I must raise me claryon voice again' the invasion iv this fair land be th' paupers an' arnychists in Europe. Ye bet I must—because I'm here first. . . . In thim days America was th' refuge iv th' oppressed in all th' wurruld. . . . But as I tell ye, 'tis diff'rent now. 'Tis time we put our back again' th' open dure an' keep out th' savage horde."

But there is no denying the fact that by the turn of the century the opinion was becoming widespread that the numbers of new immigrants should be limited. Those who were opposed to all immigration and all "foreigners" were now joined by those who believed sincerely, and with some basis in fact, that America's capacity to absorb immigration was limited. This movement toward restricting immigration represented a social and economic reaction, not only to the tremendous increase in immigration after 1880, but also to the shift in its main sources, to Southern, Eastern and Southeastern Europe.

Anti-immigration sentiment was heightened by World War I, and the disillusionment and strong wave of isolationism that marked its aftermath. It was in this climate, in 1921, that Congress passed and the President signed the first major law in our country's history severely limiting new immigration by establishing an emergency quota system. An era in American history had ended; we were committed to a radically new policy toward the peopling of the nation.

The Act of 1921 was an early version of the so-called "national origins" system. Its provisions limited immigration of numbers of each nationality to a certain percentage of the number of foreign-born individuals of that nationality resident in the United States according to the 1910 census. Nationality meant country of birth. The total number of immigrants permitted to enter under this system each year was 357,000.

In 1924 the Act was revised, creating a temporary arrangement for the years 1924 to 1929, under which the national quotas for 1924 were equal to 2 percent of the number of foreign-born persons of a given nationality living in the United States in 1890, or about 164,000 people. The permanent system, which went into force in 1929, includes essentially all the elements of immigration policy that are in our law today. The immigration statutes now establish a system of annual quotas to govern immigration from each country. Under this system 156,987 quota immigrants are permitted to enter the United States each year. The quotas from each country are based upon the national origins of the population of the United States in 1920.

The use of the year 1920 is arbitrary. It rests upon the fact that this system was introduced in 1924 and the last prior census was in 1920. The use of a national origins system is without basis in either logic or reason. It neither satisfies a national need nor accomplishes an international purpose. In an age of interdependence among nations such a system is an anachronism, for it discriminates among applicants for admission into the United States on the basis of accident of birth.

Because of the composition of our population in 1920, the system is heavily weighted in favor of immigration from Northern Europe and severely limits immigration from Southern and Eastern Europe and from other parts of the world.

To cite some recent examples: Great Britain has an annual quota of 65,361 immigration visas and used 28,291 of them. Germany has a quota of 25,814 and used 26,533 (of this number, about one-third are wives of servicemen who could enter on a nonquota basis). Ireland's quota is 17,756 and only 6,054 Irish availed themselves of it. On the other hand, Poland is permitted 6,488, and there is a backlog of 61,293 Poles wishing to enter the United States. Italy is permitted 5,666 and has a backlog of 132,435. Greece's quota is 308; her backlog is 96,538. Thus a Greek citizen desiring to emigrate to this country has little chance of coming here. And an American citizen with a Greek father or mother must wait at least eighteen months to bring his parents here to join him. A citizen whose married son or daughter, or brother or sister, is Italian cannot obtain a quota number for them for two years or more. Meanwhile, many thousands of quota numbers are wasted because they are not wanted or needed by nationals of the countries to which they are assigned.

In short, a qualified person born in England or Ireland who wants to emigrate to the United States can do so at any time. A person born in Italy, Hungary, Poland or the Baltic States may have to wait many years before his turn is reached. This system is based upon the assumption that there is some reason for keeping the origins of our population in exactly the same proportions as they existed in 1920. Such an idea is at complete variance with the American traditions and principles that the qualifications of an immigrant do not depend upon his country of birth, and violates the spirit expressed in the Declaration of Independence that "all men are created equal."

One writer has listed six motives behind the Act of 1924. They were: (1) postwar isolationism; (2) the doctrine of the alleged superiority of Anglo-Saxon and Teutonic "races"; (3) the fear that "pauper labor" would lower wage levels; (4) the belief that people of certain nations were less law-abiding than others; (5) the fear of foreign ideologies and subversion; (6) the fear that entrance of too many people with different customs and habits would undermine our national and social unity and order. All of these arguments can be found in Congressional debates on the subject and may be heard today in discussions over a new national policy toward immigration. Thus far, they have prevailed. The policy of 1924 was continued in all its essentials by the Immigration and Nationality Act of 1952.

There have been some minor amendments to that Act. In 1957 legislation was passed to reunite families being separated by restrictive provisions of the immigration legislation. Under it approximately eighty thousand persons have been admitted. Among them are the wives, husbands, parents or children of American citizens, or escapees and refugees from Communist persecution. In 1958 the immigration laws were amended to give the Attorney General added discretionary powers to adjust the status of people admitted as aliens. A 1959 amendment further facilitated the reunion of families, and a 1960 amendment provided for United States participation in the resettlement of certain refugee-escapees. In 1961 a special status was granted orphans coming to this country for adoption by American parents.

CHAPTER 7

Where We Stand

The Immigration and Nationality Act of 1952 undertook to codify all our national laws on immigration. This was a proper and long overdue task. But it was not just a housekeeping chore. In the course of the deliberation over the Act, many basic decisions about our immigration policy were made. The total racial bar against the naturalization of Japanese, Koreans and other East Asians was removed, and a minimum annual quota of one hundred was provided for each of these countries. Provision was also made to make it easier to reunite husbands and wives. Most important of all was the decision to do nothing about the national origins system.

The famous words of Emma Lazarus on the pedestal of the Statue of Liberty read: "Give me your tired, your poor, your huddled masses yearning to breathe free." Until 1921 this was an accurate picture of our society. Under present law it would be appropriate to add: "as long as they come from Northern Europe, are not too tired or too poor or slightly ill, never stole a loaf of bread, never joined any questionable organization, and can document their activities for the past two years."

Furthermore, the national origins quota system has strong overtones of an indefensible racial preference. It is strongly weighted toward so-called Anglo-Saxons, a phrase which one writer calls "a term of art" encompassing almost anyone from Northern and Western Europe. Sinclair Lewis described his hero, Martin Arrowsmith, this way: "a typical pure-bred-Anglo-Saxon American—which means that he was a union of German, French,

Scotch-Irish, perhaps a little Spanish, conceivably of the strains lumped together as 'Jewish,' and a great deal of English, which is itself a combination of primitive Britain, Celt, Phoenician, Roman, German, Dane and Swede."

Yet, however much our present policy may be deplored, it still remains our national policy. As President Truman said when he vetoed the Immigration and Nationality Act (only to have that veto overridden): "The idea behind this discriminatory policy was, to put it boldly, that Americans with English or Irish names were better people and better citizens than Americans with Italian or Greek or Polish names. . . . Such a concept is utterly unworthy of our traditions and our ideals."

Partly as a result of the inflexibility of the national origins quota system, the government has had to resort to temporary expedients to meet emergency situations. The 1957 Kennedy amendment, which permitted alien spouses, parents and children with inconsequential disqualifications to enter the United States, was responsive to this need. In 1948 Congress passed the Displaced Persons Act allowing more than 400,000 people made homeless by the war to come to this country. In 1953 Congress passed the Refugee Relief Act to admit about 200,000 people, most of whom had fled from behind the Iron Curtain. Under this Act and under a clause of the Immigration and Nationality Act of 1952, not originally intended for use in such situations, some thirty thousand Freedom Fighters from Hungary were admitted in 1957. As a result it became necessary to pass a special law in 1958 to regularize the status of many of these immigrants.

Following the 1958 earthquakes in the Azores which left so many Portuguese homeless, none of these people could enter the United States as quota immigrants. Persons of Dutch origin in the Netherlands who were displaced from Indonesia were also ineligible to enter the United States as quota immigrants. Both needs were met by the Pastore-Kennedy-Walter Act of 1958 admitting a number of them on a nonquota basis into the United States. In 1962 a special law had to be passed to permit the immigration of several thousand Chinese refugees who had escaped from Communist China to Hong Kong. The same legislative procedure was used as in the 1957 Hungarian program. Each world crisis is met by a new exception to the Immigration and Nationality Act of 1952. Each exception reflects the natural humanitarian impulses of the American people, which is in keeping with our traditions of shelter to the homeless and refuge for the oppressed.

While none of these measures are, of themselves, especially generous responses to the tremendous problems to which they are addressed, they all have a great impact on our foreign policy. They demonstrate that there is still a place in America for people fleeing from tyranny or natural calamity. Nevertheless, the effect of these actions is diluted by the very fact that they are viewed as exceptions to our national policy rather than as a part of that policy.

Another measure of the inadequacy of the Immigration and Nationality Act has been the huge volume of private immigration bills introduced in Congress. These are bills to deal with individual hardship cases for which the general law fails to provide. In the Eighty-seventh Congress over 3,500 such bills were introduced. Private immigration bills make up about half of our legislation today.

It is not hard to see why. A poor European college girl was convicted three times for putting slugs in a pay telephone, and fifteen years later, married to an American teacher abroad, she was denied entrance to our country because of three separate convictions for a crime involving moral turpitude. Or another case: An Italian immigrant living in Massachusetts with his small children could not bring his wife to the United States because she had been convicted on two counts involving moral turpitude. Her crimes? In 1913 and 1939 she had stolen bundles of sticks to build a fire. It took acts of Congress to reunite both these families.

These are examples of the inadequacies of the present law. They are important of themselves because people's lives are affected by them. But they are more important for what they represent of the way America looks at the world and the way America looks at itself.

There is, of course, a legitimate argument for some limitation upon immigration. We no longer need settlers for virgin lands, and our economy is expanding more slowly than in the nineteenth and early twentieth centuries. A superficial analysis of the heated arguments over immigration policy which have taken place since 1952 might give the impression that there was an irreconcilable conflict, as if one side wanted to go back to the policy of our founding fathers, of unrestricted immigration, and the other side wanted to stop all further immigration. In fact, there are only a few basic differences between the most liberal bill offered in recent years, sponsored by former Senator Herbert H. Lehman, and the supporters of the status quo. The present law admits 156,700 quota immigrants annually. The Lehman bill (like a bill introduced by Senator Philip A. Hart and cosponsored by over one-third of the members of the Senate) would admit 250,000.

The clash of opinion arises not over the number of immigrants to be admitted, but over the test for admission—the national origins quota system. Instead of using the discriminatory test of where the immigrant was born, the reform proposals would base admission on the immigrant's possession of skills our country needs and on the humanitarian ground of reuniting families. Such legislation does not seek to make over the face of America. Immigrants would still be given tests for health, intelligence, morality and security.

The force of this argument is recognized by the special measures enacted since 1952 which have ignored the established pattern of favoring Northern and Western Europe immigration over Southern and Eastern European countries. These statutes have resulted in the admission of a great many more persons from Southern European countries than would have been possible under the McCarran-Walter Act.

But more than a decade has elapsed since the last substantial amendment to these laws. There is a compelling need for Congress to re-examine and make changes in them.

Religious and civic organizations, ethnic associations and newspaper editorials, citizens from every walk of life and groups of every description have expressed their support for a more rational and less prejudiced immigration law. Congressional leaders of both parties have urged the adoption of new legislation that would eliminate the most objectionable features of the McCarran-Walter Act and the nationalities quota system.

It is not only the initial assignment of quota numbers which is arbitrary and unjust; additional inequity results from the failure of the law to permit full utilization of the authorized quota numbers. The tiny principality of Andorra in the Pyrenees Mountains, with 6,500 Spanish-speaking inhabitants, has an American immigration quota of 100, while Spain, with 28 million people, has a quota of only 250. While American citizens wait for years for their relatives to receive a quota, approximately sixty thousand numbers are wasted each year because the countries to which they are assigned have far more numbers allocated to them than they have emigrants seeking to move to the United States. There is no way at present in which these numbers can be reassigned to nations where immense backlogs of applicants for admission to the United States have accumulated. This deficiency in the law should be corrected.

A special discriminatory formula is now applied to the immigration of persons who are attributable by their ancestry to an area called the Asia-Pacific triangle. This area embraces all countries from Pakistan to Japan and the Pacific islands north of Australia and New Zealand. Usually, the quota under which a prospective immigrant must enter is determined by his place of birth. However, if as much as one-half of an immigrant's ancestors came from nations in the Asia-Pacific triangle, he must rely upon the small quota assigned to the country of his ancestry, regardless of where he was born. This provision of the law should be repealed.

The Presidential message to Congress of July 23, 1963, recommended that the national origins system be replaced by a formula governing immigration to the United States which takes into account: (1) the skills of the immigrant and their relationships to our needs; (2) the family relationship between immigrants and persons already here, so that the reuniting of families is encouraged; and (3) the priority of registration. Present law grants a preference to immigrants with special skills, education or training. It also grants a preference to various relatives of the United States citizens and lawfully resident aliens. But it does so only within a national origins quota. It should be modified so that those with the greatest ability to add to the national welfare, no matter where they are born, are granted the highest priority. The next priority should go to those who seek to be reunited with their relatives. For applicants with equal claims, the earliest registrant should be the first admitted.

In order to remove other existing barriers to the reuniting of families, two additional improvements in the law are needed.

First, parents of American citizens, who now have a preferred quota status, should be accorded nonquota status.

Second, parents of aliens resident in the United States, who now have no preference, should be accorded a preference, after skilled specialists and other relatives of citizens and alien residents.

These changes will have little effect on the number of immigrants admitted. They will have a major effect insofar as they relieve the hardship many of our citizens and residents now face in being separated from their parents.

These changes will not solve all the problems of immigration. But they will insure that progress will continue to be made toward our ideals and toward the realization of humanitarian objectives.

We must avoid what the Irish poet John Boyle O'Reilly once called

> Organized charity, scrimped and iced,
> In the name of a cautious, statistical Christ.

Immigration policy should be generous; it should be fair; it should be flexible. With such a policy we can turn to the world, and to our own past, with clean hands and a clear conscience. Such a policy would be but a reaffirmation of old principles. It would be an expression of our agreement with George Washington that "The bosom of America is open to receive not only the opulent and respectable stranger, but the oppressed and perse- cuted of all nations and religions; whom we shall welcome to a participation of all our rights and privileges, if by decency and propriety of conduct they appear to merit the enjoyment."

APPENDIX A

The United States of America— A Nation of Immigrants

The map on the following pages indicates the general distribution of immigrant groups in the United States. All told, more than 42 million immigrants have come to our shores since the beginning of our history as a nation. Why they came here and what they did after they arrived make up the story of America. They came for a variety of reasons from every quarter of the world, representing almost every race, almost every religion, and almost every creed. Through their ingenuity, their industry and their imagination, they were able to create out of a wilderness a thriving and prosperous nation—and, through their dedication to liberty and freedom, they helped to build a government reflecting man's most cherished ideals.

● From Great Britain came Pilgrims, who sought freedom; Quakers, who loved their brothers but who were not allowed to love them in peace; sturdy Scots and Welsh. To date, estimated immigration from Great Britain: 4,642,096. Peak year: 1888.
● The bold, imaginative Irish left their land during the years of famine for the land of opportunity. Estimated immigration from Ireland to date: 4,693,009. Peak decade: 1851–60.
● From Germany came the liberals and those who fled persecution. Estimated immigration from Germany to date: 6,798,313. Peak decade: 1881–90.
● Fleeing Czarist and Communist suppression, came an estimated 3,344,998 Russians, some 40 percent of them Jews fleeing persecution. Peak decade: 1901–10.
● Frenchmen cried, "Let us rule ourselves; our kings are not di-

vine!" To date, estimated immigration from France: 698,188. Peak year: 1851.

● The Japanese and Chinese brought their gentle dreams to the West Coast. To date, estimated immigration from Japan: 338,087. Peak year: 1907. Estimated immigration from China: 411,585. Peak year: 1882.

● The Greeks found soil where vineyards might flourish. To date, estimated immigration from Greece: 499,465. Peak year: 1907.

● In Poland they heard of the land where freedom is. To date, estimated immigration from Poland: 451,010. Peak year: 1921.

● From Austria-Hungary and Rumania whole villages banded together to find a new life. To date, estimated immigration from Austria and Hungary: 4,280,863. Peak year: 1907. To date, estimated immigration from Rumania: 159,497. Peak year: 1921.

● Italians settled in the cities of the East and the valleys of the West. To date, estimated immigration from Italy: 5,017,625. Peak year: 1907.

● To the Midwest the Scandinavians brought their knowledge of agriculture. To date, estimated immigration from Denmark: 354,331. Peak year: 1882. From Finland: 28,358. Peak year: 1902. From Norway: 843,867. Peak year: 1882. From Sweden, 1,255,296. Peak year: 1882.

These are some of yesterday's immigrants who have supplied a continuous flow of creative abilities and ideas that have enriched our nation.

The immigrants we welcome today and tomorrow will carry on this tradition and help us to retain, reinvigorate and strengthen the American spirit.

Chronology of Immigration

1607	Founding of Virginia by English colonists, to "fetch treasure" and enjoy "religious and happy government."
1619	First shipload of twenty Negro slaves arrives at Jamestown.
1620	Voyage of the *Mayflower*, carrying Pilgrims who welcome opportunity of "advancing the gospel of . . . Christ in those remote parts of the world."
1623	Settlement of New Netherland as a trading post by Dutch West India Company.
1630–40	Puritans migrate to New England to establish a form of government that will allow them to worship as they desire.
1634	Lord Baltimore founds Maryland as a refuge for English Catholics.
1642	Outbreak of English Civil War and decrease in Puritan migration.
1649	Passage of Maryland Toleration Act, extending toleration to all bodies professing trinitarian Christianity.
1654	First Jewish immigrants to reach North America arrive at New Amsterdam fleeing Portuguese persecution in Brazil.
1660	Emigration from England officially discouraged by government of Charles II, acting on mercantilist doctrine that the wealth of a country depends on number of its inhabitants.
1670	Settlement of the Carolinas by a group of English courtiers, anxious to promote national self-sufficiency—and their own fortunes.
1681	Founding of Pennsylvania by the Quakers, as William Penn's "holy experiment" in universal philanthropy and brotherhood.
1683	First German settlers, Mennonites, to reach New World arrive in Pennsylvania, in a desire to withdraw from the

world and live peaceably according to the tenets of their faith.

1685   Revocation of Edict of Nantes by Louis XIV, culmination of growth of religious intolerance in France, leads to arrival of small but important group of Huguenots. Most settle in South Carolina.

1697   Royal African Company's monopoly of slave trade ends and the business of slavery expands rapidly. New Englanders find it extremely profitable.

1707   Act of Union between England and Scotland begins a new era of Scottish migration. Scots settle as merchants and factors in colonial seaports; lowland artisans and laborers leave Glasgow to become indentured servants in tobacco colonies and New York.

1709   Exodus from German Palatinate in wake of devastation wreaked by wars of Louis XIV. Palatines settle in Hudson Valley and Pennsylvania.

1717   Act of English Parliament legalizes transportation to American colonies as punishment; contractors begin regular shipments from jails, most (of some 30,000) to Virginia and Maryland.

1718   Large-scale Scotch-Irish immigration begins, sparked by discontent with Old Country land system: absentee landlords, high rents, short leases. Most settle first in New England, then in Maryland and Pennsylvania.

1730   Colonization of Virginia valley and Carolina back country by Germans (Pietist and pacifist sectarians) and Scotch-Irish from Pennsylvania.

1732   Georgia founded by James Oglethorpe, as a buffer against Spanish and French attack, as a producer of raw silk and as a haven for imprisoned debtors. (Silk scheme fails; only a handful of debtors come.)

1740   Parliament enacts Naturalization Act conferring British citizenship on alien immigrants to colonies in hope of encouraging Jewish immigration. Jews enjoy a greater degree of political and religious freedom in the American colonies than anywhere in the world.

1745   Jacobite rebellion in Scotland to put Stuarts back on throne fails. Some rebels transported to American colonies as punishment.

1755   Expulsion of French Acadians from Nova Scotia on suspicion
            of disloyalty. Survivors settle in Louisiana.

1771–73   Depression in Ulster linen trade and acute agrarian crisis
            bring new influx of Scotch-Irish, around 10,000 annually.

1775   British Government suspends emigration on outbreak of
            hostilities in America.

1783   Treaty of Paris ends Revolutionary War. Revival of im-
            migration; most numerous group: Scotch-Irish.

1789   Outbreak of French Revolution. Emigration to the United
            States of aristocrats and royalist sympathizers.

1791   Negro revolt in Santo Domingo; 10,000–20,000 French
            exiles take refuge in the United States, principally in towns
            on the Atlantic seaboard.

1793   Wars of the French Revolution send Girondists and Jacobins
            threatened by guillotine to the United States.

1798   Unsuccessful Irish rebellion; rebels emigrate to U.S., as do
            distressed artisans and yeoman farmers and agricultural
            laborers depressed by bad harvests and low prices.

            Alien and Sedition Acts give President arbitrary powers to
            seize and expel resident aliens suspected of engaging in
            subversive activities. Though never invoked, Acts induce
            several shiploads of Frenchmen to return to France and
            Santo Domingo.

1803   Resumption of war between England and France. Disruption
            of transatlantic trade; emigration from continental Europe
            practically impossible.

            British Passenger Act limits numbers to be carried by
            emigrant ships, effectively checks Irish emigration.

1807   Congress prohibits importing of Negro slaves into the U.S.
            (prohibited by Delaware in 1776; Virginia, 1778; Maryland,
            1783; South Carolina, 1787; North Carolina, 1794; Georgia,
            1798; reopened by South Carolina in 1803).

1812   War of 1812 brings immigration to a complete halt.

1814   Treaty of Ghent ends War of 1812. Beginning of first great
            wave of immigration: 5,000,000 immigrants between 1815
            and 1860.

1818   Black Ball Line of sailing packets begins regular Liverpool–
            New York service; Liverpool becomes main port of departure
            for Irish and British, as well as considerable numbers of
            Germans and Norwegians.

1825   Great Britain repeals laws prohibiting emigration as in-
          effective; official endorsement of view that England is over-
          populated.
             Arrival in U.S. of first group of Norwegian immigrants in
          sloop *Restaurationen,* consisting of freeholders leaving an
          overpopulated country and shrunken farms. They are fol-
          lowed by cotters, laborers and servants.

1830   Polish revolution. Thirty-six sections of public land in Illi-
          nois allotted by Congress to Polish revolutionary refugees.

1837   Financial panic. Nativists complain that immigration lowers
          wage levels, contributes to the decline of the apprenticeship
          system and generally depresses the condition of labor.

1840   Cunard Line founded. Beginning of era of steamship lines
          especially designed for passenger transportation between
          Europe and the United States.

1845   Native American party founded, with minimal support in
          fourteen states; precursor of nativist, anti-immigrant Know-
          Nothing party which reached its peak in 1855, when it
          elected six governors, dominated several state legislatures and
          sent a sizable delegation to Congress.

1846   Crop failures in Germany and Holland. Mortgage fore-
          closures and forced sales send tens of thousands of dis-
          possessed to U.S.

1846–47   Irish potato famine. Large-scale emigration to the United
          States of all classes of Irish population, not only laborers
          and cotters, but even substantial farmers.

1848   Revolution in Germany. Failure of revolution results in
          emigration of political refugees to America.

1855   Opening of Castle Garden immigrant depot in New York
          City to process mass immigration.

1856   Collapse of Know-Nothing movement in Presidential election;
          candidate Millard Fillmore carries only one state.
             Irish Catholic Colonization Convention at Buffalo, New
          York, to promote Irish rural colonization in the U.S. Strongly
          opposed by Eastern bishops, movement proves unsuccessful.

1861–65   Large numbers of immigrants serve on both sides during
          American Civil War.

1882   First federal immigration law bars lunatics, idiots, convicts
          and those likely to become public charges.
             Chinese Exclusion Act denies entry to Chinese laborers

for a period of ten years (renewed in 1892; Chinese immigration suspended indefinitely in 1902; many return home).
Outbreak of anti-Semitism in Russia; sharp rise in Jewish migration to U.S.

1885   Foran Act prohibits importing of contract labor, but not of skilled labor for new industries, artists, actors, lecturers, domestic servants; individuals in U.S. not to be prevented from assisting immigration of relatives and personal friends.

1886   Statue of Liberty dedicated, just when the resistance to unrestricted immigration begins to mount.

1890   Superintendent of the Census announces disappearance of the frontier.

1891   Congress adds health qualifications to immigration restrictions.
Pogroms in Russia. Large Jewish immigration to U.S.

1892   Ellis Island replaces Castle Garden as a reception center for immigrants.

1893   Economic depression brings a vast accession of strength to anti-Catholic American Protective Association.

1894   Immigration Restriction League organized, to be the spearhead of restrictionist movement for next twenty-five years. Emphasizes distinction between "old" (Northern and Western European) and "new" (Southern and Eastern European) immigrants.

1894–96 Massacres of Armenian Christians by Moslems set emigration to U.S. in motion.

1897   Literacy test for immigrants vetoed by President Cleveland.

1903   Immigration law denies entry, *inter alia,* to anarchists or persons believing in the overthrow by force or violence of the government of the U.S., or any government, or in the assassination of public officials (as a result of President McKinley's assassination by the American-born anarchist Leon Czolgosz).

1905   Japanese and Korean Exclusion League formed by organized labor in protest against influx of coolie labor and in fear of threat to the living standards of American workingmen.

1907–08 Gentleman's agreement, whereby Japanese Government undertakes to deny passports to laborers going directly from Japan to U.S., fails to satisfy West Coast exclusionists.

1913   California legislature passes Alien Land Law, effectively barring Japanese, as "aliens ineligible for citizenship," from owning agricultural land in the state.

1914–18 World War I. End of period of mass migration to the U.S.

1916 Madison Grant's *The Passing of the Great Race* calls for exclusion, on racist grounds, of "inferior" Alpine, Mediterranean and Jewish "breeds."

1917 Literacy test for immigrants finally adopted after being defeated in Congress in 1896, 1898, 1902, 1906, vetoed in 1897 by President Cleveland, in 1913 by President Taft, and in 1915 and 1917 by President Wilson. It was passed by overriding the second veto by President Wilson.

1919 Big Red scare: anti-foreign fears and hatreds transferred from German Americans to alien revolutionaries and radicals. Thousands of alien radicals seized in Palmer raids, hundreds deported.

1921 Emergency immigration restriction law introduces quota system, heavily weighted in favor of natives of Northern and Western Europe, all but slamming the door on Southern and Eastern Europeans. Immediate slump in immigration.

1923 Ku Klux Klan, at heart a virulently anti-immigrant movement, reaches its peak strength.

1924 National Origins Act adopted, settling ceiling on number of immigrants, and establishing discriminatory national-racial quotas.

1929 National Origins Act becomes operative. Stock market crash. Demands that immigration be further reduced during economic crisis lead Hoover administration to order rigorous enforcement of prohibition against admission of persons liable to be public charges.

1933 Hitler becomes German chancellor; anti-Semitic campaign begins. Jewish refugees from Nazi Germany come to U.S., though barriers imposed by the quota system are not lifted.

1934 Philippine Independence Act restricts Filipino immigration to an annual quota of fifty.

1939 World War II begins.

1941 U.S. enters war. All immigrant groups support united war effort.

1942 Evacuation of Japanese-Americans from Pacific Coast to detention camps, victims of deep-seated suspicion and animosity, and unjustified fear of espionage and sabotage.

1945   Large-scale Puerto Rican migration to escape poverty on island. Many settle in New York.

1946   War Brides Act provides for admission of foreign-born wives of American servicemen.

1948   Displaced Persons Act (amended in 1950) provides for admission of 400,000 refugees during a four-year period: three-quarters regular displaced persons from countries with low quotas, one-quarter *Volksdeutsche* (ethnic Germans), special groups of Greek, Polish and Italian refugees, orphans and European refugees stranded in the Far East.

1952   Immigration and Naturalization Act, codifying existing legislation, makes the quota system even more rigid and repressive, except for a token quota granted those in the Asia-Pacific triangle.

1953–56 Refugee Relief Act grants visas to some 5,000 Hungarians after 1956 revolution; President Eisenhower invites 30,000 more to come in on parole.

1954   Ellis Island closed. Symbol of ending of mass migration.

1957   Special legislation to admit Hungarian refugees.

1959   Castro revolution successful in Cuba.

1960   Cuban refugees paroled into U.S.

1962   Special permission for admission of refugees from Hong Kong.

1963   Congress urged by President Kennedy to pass new legislation eliminating national origins quota system.

APPENDIX C

🏴

Suggested Reading

🏴

The following bibliography is in no way inclusive. Although many of the books overlap in subject matter, an effort has been made to organize them under three categories: General; Studies in Specialized Areas; and Minorities in America.

GENERAL

BEARD, ANNIE E. S. *Our Foreign-Born Citizens*. New York: Crowell, 1955. Short biographies of well-known Americans of foreign birth.

BERNARD, WILLIAM S., et al., eds. *American Immigration Policy*. New York: Harper, 1950. Describes the origins and effects of the quota system.

BOWERS, DAVID F., ed. *Foreign Influences in American Life*. Princeton: Princeton University Press, 1944. Exploratory essays on the development of the immigrant.

BROWN, FRANCIS J., and ROUČEK, JOSEPH S. *One America*. New York: Prentice-Hall, 1952. The history, contributions and present problems of religious, ethnic and racial groups in America.

BRUCE, CAMPBELL J. *The Golden Door*. New York: Random House, 1954. Case studies of the present effects of immigration and deportation policies.

COLE, STEWART G., and COLE, MILDRED WIESE. *Minorities and the American Promise*. New York: Harper, 1954. Discusses the relations of 180 million Americans of many racial, religious and national stocks.

COMMAGER, HENRY STEELE, ed. *Immigration and American History*. Minneapolis: University of Minnesota Press, 1961. Essays discussing a number of aspects of American immigration.

CORSI, EDWARD. *In the Shadow of Liberty*. New York: Macmillan, 1935.

The story of Ellis Island told by the first United States Commissioner of Immigration.

DIVINE, ROBERT A. *American Immigration Policy, 1924–1952*. New Haven: Yale, 1957. A comprehensive treatment of immigration policy.

EATON, ALLEN H. *Immigrant Gifts to American Life*. New York: Russell Sage Foundation, 1932. Contributions of our foreign-born citizens to American cultural development.

GAUSTAD, EDWIN SCOTT. *Historical Atlas of Religion in America*. New York: Harper, 1962. A compilation of maps, charts and other data descriptive of the growth of major religious groups in America.

GLAZER, NATHAN, and MOYNIHAN, DANIEL. *Beyond the Melting Pot*. Cambridge: M.I.T., 1963. Negroes, Puerto Ricans, Jews, Italians and Irish of New York City.

GUILLET, EDWIN C. *The Great Migration: The Atlantic Crossing by Sailing Ship Since 1770*. New York: Nelson, 1937. Dramatic description of conditions in port cities at both ends of the immigrant journey and aboard ship.

HANDLIN, OSCAR. *The Americans*. Boston: Little, Brown, 1963. Discusses the gradual unfolding of the American character.

——— (ed.). *Immigration as a Factor in American History*. New York: Spectrum Books, Prentice-Hall, 1959.

——— (ed.). *This Was America*. Cambridge: Harvard, 1949 (Harper Torchbooks). True accounts as recorded by European travelers in the eighteenth, nineteenth and twentieth centuries.

———. *The Uprooted*. Boston: Atlantic Monthly Press, 1951 (Universal Library). The story of the great migrations that made the American people.

HANSEN, MARCUS LEE. *The Atlantic Migration, 1607–1860*. Cambridge: Harvard, 1940 (Harper Torchbooks). The origins and transfer of immigrants from Europe to the United States.

———. *The Immigrant in American History*. Cambridge: Harvard, 1940 (Harper Torchbooks). Interpretive essays on the immigration contribution.

HIGHAM, JOHN. *Strangers in the Land*. New Brunswick: Rutgers, 1955 (Atheneum Paperbacks). Patterns of American nativism, 1860–1925.

HUTCHINSON, E. P. *Immigrants and Their Children, 1850–1950*. New York: Wiley, 1956. A statistical study of adjustments of various immigrant groups and their descendants.

JAWORSKI, IRENE D. *Becoming American.* New York: Harper, 1960. Describes the various problems the immigrant encounters in adjusting to American life.

JONES, MALDWYN ALLEN. *American Immigration.* Chicago: University of Chicago Press, 1960. Traces the impact of immigrants on American culture, politics, and economic growth.

MAISEL, ALBERT Q. *They All Chose America.* New York: Nelson, 1957. A popular account of the various nationalities who came to America.

POTTER, GEORGE. *To the Golden Door.* Boston: Little, Brown, 1960. Story of the Irish in Ireland and America.

SCHERMERHORN, R. A. *These Our People: Minorities in American Culture.* New York: Heath, 1949. One-chapter treatments of five immigrant groups: Italians, Poles, Czechs and Slovaks, Hungarians and Yugoslavians.

SCHLESINGER, ARTHUR M. *Paths to the Present.* New York: Macmillan, 1949 (Sentry Editions, Houghton Mifflin). Discusses various phases of immigration, including the role of the immigrant in shaping American ideals.

SENIOR, CLARENCE. *Strangers Then Neighbors: From Pilgrims to Puerto Ricans.* New York: Anti-Defamation League, 1961. Examines the pattern and history of immigration to the U.S., with emphasis on the significance of recent Puerto Rican migration.

SMITH, WILLIAM CARLSON. *Americans in the Making: The Natural History of the Assimilation of Immigrants.* New York: Appleton-Century, 1939. Describes the process of individual adjustment through which the immigrant typically passed.

STEPHENSON, GEORGE M. *A History of American Immigration—1820–1924.* Boston: Ginn, 1926. A discussion of immigration as a factor in American political development.

TAFT and ROBBINS. *International Migrations, The Immigrant in the Modern World.* New York: Ronald Press, 1955. Discusses migration as one of the many threads interwoven in a changing pattern of social relations among men.

WITTKE, CARL. *We Who Built America: The Saga of the Immigrant.* Cleveland: Western Reserve University Press, 1939. Storehouse of information on various aspects of immigration.

WOODHAM-SMITH, CECIL. *The Great Hunger.* New York: Harper, 1963 (Signet Books). The conditions in Ireland that led to mass immigration to the United States.

STUDIES IN SPECIALIZED AREAS

ABBOTT, EDITH, ed. *Historical Aspects of the Immigration Problem.*
Chicago: University of Chicago Press, 1926. Select documents re-
lating to immigration.

BILLINGTON, RAY ALLEN. *The Protestant Crusade, 1800–1860: A
Study of the Origins of American Nativism.* New York: Macmillan,
1938 (Quadrangle Books). A study of anti-Catholic propaganda in
the nineteenth century.

BLEGEN, THEODORE C., ed. *Land of Their Choice: The Immigrants
Write Home.* Minneapolis: University of Minnesota Press, 1955. Collection of letters of immigrants describing their life in this country.

BOORSTIN, DANIEL J. *The Americans: The Colonial Experience.* New
York: Random House, 1958. Impact of the American environment
upon the various groups of colonists.

CHILDS, FRANCES S. *French Refugee Life in the United States, 1790–
1800.* Baltimore: Johns Hopkins, 1940. Describes an American chapter of the French Revolution.

CRAVEN, WESLEY F. *The Legend of the Founding Fathers.* New York:
New York University Press, 1956. Origins of the Puritan migrations.

ERICKSON, CHARLOTTE. *American Industry and the European Immigrant, 1860–1885.* Cambridge: Harvard, 1957. A study of the immigrant's effects on American industrialization.

ERNST, ROBERT. *Immigrant Life in New York City, 1825–1863.* New
York: King's Crown Press, 1949. The intermingling of various
groups during the mid-nineteenth century.

GATES, PAUL W. *The Illinois Central Railroad and Its Colonization
Work.* Cambridge: Harvard, 1934. The activities of the railroads in
colonization.

HANDLIN, OSCAR. *Danger in Discord.* New York: Anti-Defamation
League, 1948. Origins of anti-Semitism in the United States.

———. *Boston's Immigrants, 1790–1865; A Study in Acculturation.*
Cambridge: Harvard, 1941. Describes the "Yankee" hostility to immigration in Boston.

JANSON, FLORENCE EDITH. *The Background of Swedish Immigration,
1840–1930.* Chicago: University of Chicago Press, 1931. The impulses which sent the Swedes to the United States.

KORN, BERTRAM WALLACE. *American Jewry and the Civil War.* New
York: Meridian Paperbacks, 1951. Includes a study of the outbreak
of anti-Semitism during this period.

KRAUS, MICHAEL. *The Atlantic Civilization: Eighteenth-century*

Origins. New York: Van Nostrand, Anvil Books, 1949. A study of cultural exchange among the various Atlantic countries.

MARCUS, JACOB R. *Early American Jewry*. Philadelphia: Jewish Publication Society, 1951. An account of the Jews in the colonial period in New York, New England and Canada.

MULDER, WILLIAM. *Homeward to Zion*. Minneapolis: University of Minnesota Press, 1957. The Norman migration from Scandinavia.

MURRAY, ROBERT K. *Red Scare: A Study in National Hysteria, 1919–1920*. Minneapolis: University of Minnesota Press, 1955 (McGraw-Hill Paperback Series). Evaluation of the Palmer raids and other manifestations of this period.

NEVINS, ALLAN, and HILL, FRANK E. *Ford: Expansion and Challenge* (2nd volume of a 3-volume work). New York: Scribner, 1957. Covers Ford's venture into anti-Semitism.

PHILLIPS, ULRICH BONNELL. *American Negro Slavery*. Gloucester: Peter Smith, 1959. A discussion of aspects of the slave trade.

RISCHIN, MOSES. *The Promised City*. Cambridge: Harvard, 1962. Jewish community life in New York City, 1870–1914.

SALOUTOS, THEODORE. *They Remember America*. Berkeley: University of California Press, 1956. The story of repatriated Greek-Americans.

SANDMEYER, ELMER C. *The Anti-Chinese Movement in California*. Urbana: University of Illinois Press, 1939. Traces the growth of nativism in California.

SCHRIER, ARNOLD. *Ireland and American Emigration, 1850–1900*. Minneapolis: University of Minnesota Press, 1958. American influences which filtered back to Ireland.

SMITH, ABBOTT E. *Colonists in Bondage: White Servitude and Convict Labor in America, 1607–1776*. Chapel Hill: University of North Carolina Press, 1947. A treatment of the problem of indentured servants who came to America.

SMITH, JAMES MORTON. *Freedom's Fetters*. Ithaca: Cornell, 1956. The Alien and Sedition Acts and American civil liberties.

SOLOMON, BARBARA. *Ancestors and Immigrants*. Cambridge: Harvard, 1956. A study of New England nativism.

TUPPER and McREYNOLDS. *Japan in American Public Opinion*. New York: George H. Blakeslee, 1937. Traces American antipathies to Japanese migration.

WITTKE, CARL F. *The German-Language Press in America*. Lexington: University of Kentucky Press, 1957. The influence of German newspapers on American life.

———. *Refugees of Revolution: The German Forty-Eighters in America*. Philadelphia: University of Pennsylvania Press, 1952. A study of the people who fled Germany at the time of the revolutions of 1848.

MINORITIES IN AMERICA

BENSON and HADIN. *Americans from Sweden*. Philadelphia: Lippincott, 1950.

BERTHOFF, ROWLAND T. *British Immigrants in Industrial America, 1790–1950*. Cambridge: Harvard, 1953.

BLEGEN, THEODORE C. *Norwegian Migration to America, 1825–1860*. Northfield, Minn.: Norwegian-American History Association, 1940.

BURMA, JOHN H. *Spanish-Speaking Groups in the United States*. Durham: Duke, 1954.

CONWAY, ALAN, ed. *The Welsh in America; Letters from Immigrants*. Minneapolis: University of Minnesota Press, 1961.

DAVIS, JEROME D. *The Russian Immigrant*. New York: Macmillan, 1922.

FAUST, ALBERT B. *The German Element in the United States*. 2 vols. New York: Houghton, 1909.

FOERSTER, ROBERT F. *The Italian Emigration of Our Time*. Cambridge: Harvard, 1919.

FOSDICK, LUCIAN J. *The French Blood in America*. Boston: Gorham Press, 1919.

GINZBERG, ELI, and EICHNER, ALFRED S. *The Troublesome Presence: American Democracy and the Negro*. New York: Free Press, 1964.

GOVORCHIN, G. G. *Americans from Yugoslavia*. Gainesville: University of Florida Press, 1961.

GRAHAM, IAN. *Colonists from Scotland*. Ithaca: Cornell, 1956.

HANDLIN, OSCAR. *Adventure in Freedom*. New York: McGraw-Hill, 1954. Discusses three hundred years of Jewish life in America.

HANSEN, MARCUS LEE. *The Mingling of the Canadian and American Peoples*. New Haven: Yale, 1940.

HAWGOOD, JOHN A. *The Tragedy of German-America; The Germans in the United States of America during the Nineteenth Century—and After*. Toronto: T. Allen, 1940.

HITTI, PHILIP K. *The Syrians in America*. New York: George H. Doran, 1924.

HOGLUND, WILLIAM A. *Finnish Immigrants in America*. Madison: University of Wisconsin Press, 1960.

ICHIHASHI, YAMATO. *Japanese in the United States*. Stanford: Stanford University Press, 1932.

LEARSI, RUFUS. *Jews in America, A History*. Cleveland: World, 1954.

LEE, ROSE HUM. *The Chinese in the United States of America*. London: Oxford, 1960.

LENGYEL, EMIL. *Americans from Hungary*. Philadelphia: Lippincott, 1948.

LEYBURN, JAMES. *The Scotch-Irish: A Social History*. Chapel Hill: University of North Carolina Press, 1962.

LUCAS, HENRY S. *Netherlanders in America*. Ann Arbor: University of Michigan Press, 1955.

MALCOLM, M. VARTON. *The Armenians in America*. Boston: Pilgrim Press, 1912.

MCWILLIAMS, CAREY. *North from Mexico*. New York: Monthly Review Press, 1961.

MILLS, SENIOR, KOHN and GOLDSEN. *The Puerto Rican Journey*. New York: Harper, 1950.

REID, IRA DE AUGUSTINE. *The Negro Immigrant, His Background, Characteristics, and Social Adjustment*. New York: Columbia, 1939.

SALOUTOS, THEODORE. *The Greeks in the U.S.* Cambridge: Harvard, 1963.

SHANNON, WILLIAM V. *The American Irish*. New York: Macmillan, 1963.

SMITH, BRADFORD. *Americans from Japan*. Philadelphia: Lippincott, 1948.

WITTKE, CARL F. *The Irish in America*. Baton Rouge: Louisiana State, 1956.

WYTRWAL, JOSEPH A. *America's Polish Heritage*. Detroit: Endurance Press, 1961.

Text of President John F. Kennedy's Proposals to Liberalize Immigration Statutes

(JULY 23, 1963)

I am transmitting herewith, for the consideration of the Congress, legislation revising and modernizing our immigration laws. More than a decade has elapsed since the last substantial amendment to these laws. I believe there exists a compelling need for the Congress to re-examine and make certain changes in these laws.

The most urgent and fundamental reform I am recommending relates to the national origins system of selecting immigrants. Since 1924 it has been used to determine the number of quota immigrants permitted to enter the United States each year. Accordingly, although the legislation I am transmitting deals with many problems which require remedial action, it concentrates attention primarily upon revision of our quota immigration system. The enactment of this legislation will not resolve all of our important problems in the field of immigration law. It will, however, provide a sound basis upon which we can build in developing an immigration law that serves the national interest and reflects in every detail the principles of equality and human dignity to which our nation subscribes.

ELIMINATION OF DISCRIMINATION BASED ON NATIONAL ORIGINS

Present legislation establishes a system of annual quotas to govern immigration from each country. Under this system, 156,700 quota immigrants are permitted to enter the United States each year. The system is based upon the national origins of the population of the United States in 1920. The use of the year 1920 is arbitrary. It rests upon the fact that this system was introduced in 1924 and the last prior census was in 1920. The use of a national origins system is without basis in either logic or reason. It neither satisfies a national need nor accomplishes an international purpose. In an age of interdependence among nations, such a system is an anachronism, for it discriminates among applicants for admission into the United States on the basis of accident of birth.

Because of the composition of our population in 1920, the system is heavily weighted in favor of immigration from northern Europe and severely limits immigration from southern and eastern Europe and from other parts of the world. An American citizen with a Greek father or mother must wait at least eighteen months to bring his parents here to join him. A citizen whose married son or daughter, or brother or sister, is Italian cannot obtain a quota number for an even longer time. Meanwhile, many thousands of quota numbers are wasted because they are not wanted or needed by nationals of the countries to which they are assigned.

I recommend that there be substituted for the national origins system a formula governing immigration to the United States which takes into account (1) the skills of the immigrant and their relationship to our need; (2) the family relationship between immigrants and persons already here, so that the reuniting of families is encouraged and (3) the priority of registration. Present law grants a preference to immigrants with special skills, education or training. It also grants a preference to various relatives of United States citizens and lawfully resident aliens. But it does so only within a national origins quota. It should be modified so that those with the greatest ability to add to the national welfare, no matter where they were born, are granted the highest priority. The next priority should go to those who seek to be reunited with their relatives. As between applicants with equal claims the earliest registrant should be the first admitted.

Many problems of fairness and foreign policy are involved in replacing a system so long entrenched. The national origins system has produced large backlogs of applications in some countries, and too rapid a change might, in a system of limited immigration, so drastically curtail immigration in some countries the only effect might be to shift the unfairness from one group of nations to another. A reasonable time to adjust to any new system must be provided if individual hardships upon persons who were relying on the present system are to be avoided. In addition, any new system must have sufficient flexibility to allow adjustments to be made when it appears that immigrants from nations closely allied to the United States will be unduly restricted in their freedom to furnish the new seed population that has so long been a source of strength to our nation.

PROPOSAL IN DETAIL

Accordingly, I recommend:

First, that existing quotas be reduced gradually, at the rate of 20 percent a year. The quota numbers released each year would be placed in a quota reserve pool, to be distributed on the new basis.

Second, that natives of no one country receive over 10 percent of the total quota numbers authorized in any one year. This will insure that the pattern of immigration is not distorted by excessive demand from any one country.

Third, that the President be authorized, after receiving recommendations from a seven-man Immigration Board, to reserve up to 50 percent of the unallocated quota numbers for issuance to persons disadvantaged by the change in the quota system, and up to 20 percent to refugees whose sudden dislocation requires special treatment. The Immigration Board will be composed of two members appointed by the Speaker of the House of Representatives, two members appointed by the President Pro Tempore of the Senate, and three members appointed by the President. In addition to its responsibility for formulating recommendations regarding the use of the quota reserve pool, the Board will make a continuous study of our immigration policy.

ALL QUOTA NUMBERS USED

But it is not alone the initial assignment of quota numbers which is arbitrary and unjust; additional inequity results from the failure of the law to permit full utilization of the authorized quota numbers. While American citizens wait for years for their relatives to receive a quota, approximately sixty thousand quota numbers are wasted each year because the countries to which they are assigned have far more numbers allocated to them than they have emigrants seeking to move to the United States. There is no way at present in which these numbers can be reassigned to nations where immense backlogs of applicants for admission to the United States have accumulated. I recommend that this deficiency in the law be corrected.

ASIA-PACIFIC TRIANGLE

A special discriminatory formula is now used to regulate the immigration of persons who are attributable by their ancestry to an area called the Asia-Pacific triangle. This area embraces all countries from Pakistan to Japan and the Pacific islands north of Australia and New Zealand. Usually, the quota under which a prospective immigrant must enter is determined by his place of birth. However, if as much as one-half of an immigrant's ancestors came from nations in the Asia-Pacific triangle, he must rely upon the small quota assigned to the country of his ancestry, regardless of where he was born. This provision of our law should be repealed.

OTHER PROVISIONS

In order to remove other existing barriers to the reuniting of families, I recommend two additional improvements in the law.

First, parents of American citizens, who now have a preferred quota status, should be accorded nonquota status.

Second, parents of aliens resident in the United States, who now have no preference, should be accorded a preference, after skilled specialists and other relatives of citizens and alien residents.

These changes will have little effect on the number of immigrants admitted. They will have a major effect upon the individual hardships many of our citizens and residents now face in being separated from their parents.

In addition, I recommend the following changes in the law in order to correct certain deficiencies and improve its general application.

1. Changes in the Preference Structure. At present, the procedure under which specially skilled or trained workers are permitted to enter this country too often prevents talented people from applying for visas to enter the United States. It often deprives us of immigrants who would be helpful to our economy and our culture. This procedure should be liberalized so that highly trained or skilled persons may obtain a preference without requiring that they secure employment here before emigrating. In addition, I recommend that a special preference be accorded workers with lesser skills who can fill specific needs in short supply in this country.

2. Nonquota status for natives of Jamaica, Trinidad and Tobago should be granted. Under existing law, no numerical limitation is imposed upon the number of immigrants coming from Canada, Mexico,

Cuba, Haiti, the Dominican Republic, the Canal Zone or any independent country in Central or South America. But the language of the statute restricts this privilege to persons born in countries in the Caribbean area which gained their independence prior to the date of the last major amendment to the immigration and nationality statutes, in 1952. This accidental discrimination against the newly independent nations of the Western Hemisphere should be corrected.

3. Persons afflicted with mental health problems should be admitted provided certain standards are met. Today, any person afflicted with a mental disease or mental defect, psychotic personality, or epilepsy, and any person who has suffered an attack of mental illness, can enter this country only if a private bill is enacted for his benefit. Families which are able and willing to care for a mentally ill child or parent are often forced to choose between living in the United States and leaving their loved ones behind and not living in the United States but being able to see and care for their loved ones. Mental illness is not incurable. It should be treated like other illnesses. I recommend that the Attorney General, at his discretion and under proper safeguards, be authorized to waive those provisions of the law which prohibit the admission to the United States of persons with mental problems when they are close relatives of United States citizens and lawfully resident aliens.

4. The Secretary of State should be authorized, in his discretion, to require re-registration of certain quota immigrant visa applicants and to regulate the time of payment of visa fees. This authority would bring registration lists up to date, terminate the priority of applicants who have refused to accept a visa, and end the problem of "insurance" registrations by persons who have no present intention to emigrate. Registration figures for oversubscribed quota areas are now inaccurate because there exists no way of determining whether registrants have died, have emigrated to other countries, or for some other reason no longer want to emigrate to the United States. These problems are particularly acute in heavily oversubscribed areas.

CONCLUSION

As I have already indicated the measures I have outlined will not solve all the problems of immigration. Many of them will require additional legislation; some cannot be solved by any one country. But the legislation I am submitting will insure that progress will continue to be made toward our ideals and toward the realization of humanitarian objectives. The measures I have recommended will help eliminate discrimination between peoples and nations on a basis that is unrelated to any contribution that immigrants can make and is inconsistent with our traditions of welcome. Our investment in new citizens has always been a valuable source of our strength.

APPENDIX E

Selected Comments on President Kennedy's Message

Senator Philip A. Hart, Democrat of Michigan, speaking of the message on revision of the immigration laws sent to the Congress in 1963, said:

> It is fitting that this proposal should come at a time when the nation and the Congress are deeply committed to a full review of our practices and laws affecting our fellow citizens of different races. . . . Let us get on with this job.

From the other side of the chamber, Republican Senator Kenneth B. Keating of New York declared:

> I am very pleased that the executive branch has now made these proposals and I am sympathetic to the approach in this bill. . . . I shall certainly exert every possible effort to have such legislation enacted at this session . . . and hope that there will be prompt hearings on this important subject.

Strong support for a thoroughgoing revision of our present immigration policy came from Senator Hubert H. Humphrey, the Minnesota Democrat. He said:

> Although Congress faces many urgent matters of national importance at this session and the next, I fervently hope we can nevertheless push ahead with the long-postponed, long-overdue task of bringing our immigration laws up to the civilized standard which the world has reason to expect of the United States. The present system is cruel, unworkable, discriminatory, and illogical.

Republican Senator Hiram L. Fong of Hawaii said: "I shall strongly support efforts to basically revise our immigration laws and policies," and added that he was "heartened" by the administration's recognition of the need for a basic change in American immigration policies.

Congressman Emanuel Celler of New York, Chairman of the House Judiciary Committee, said:

It is my considered opinion that the President's bill offers a broad and firm basis for a long overdue revision of our policies and practices in this most important area of domestic and foreign human relations.

Congressman James Roosevelt of California stated:

The President of the United States has urgently called upon the Congress to implement long overdue and sorely needed changes in our immigration laws.

I would like to strongly urge my colleagues to join with me in supporting this new and far reaching immigration proposal of the President's.

Congressman William F. Ryan of New York said:

I believe that President Kennedy's proposals represent a giant step forward in the creation of a sensible and humane immigration policy.

Newspaper editorials reflected a similar, nonpartisan approach to the projected revisions. The Chicago *Tribune* commented:

The idea of shifting the basis of immigrants' admission from the arbitrary one of country of origin to the rational and humane ones of occupational skills and reuniting families deserves approval.

The policy of action without regard to race, religion, or country of origin has increasing appeal and scope in the United States, especially in the processes of government. The immigration quotas have been the principal exception in federal practice to equality before the law for people whatever the circumstances of their birth. It is an exception that it is well to reconsider.

The Denver *Post* approvingly said of the proposed changes:

It would replace a system based on racial and national discrimination with one having two worthwhile and humane objectives: to assure the United States of a continuing flow of usefully-skilled new citizens, and to reunite the families of U.S. citizens.

The Washington *Post*, July 24, 1963, called President Kennedy's proposal "the best immigration law within living memory to bear a White House endorsement."

The *New York Times*, July 25, 1963, in its lead editorial stated:

> . . . Adoption of the President's wise recommendations would be an act of justice and wisdom, as well as evidence that we fully understand the true nature of the changed world—now grown so small—in which all humanity lives.

The St. Paul *Pioneer Press* editorialized on July 26, 1963:

> Possibly the only negative feature of the administration's new immigration plan is the five years it proposes to take in implementing it. The present system is so archaic and inflexible as to deserve speedier abandonment.

"It is time to lay aside the thinking of the '20s in favor of the realities of the '60s with regard to our unreasonable quota system on immigration," wrote the Chattanooga *Times*. It continued:

> The system of national quotas has long been recognized as a paradox, in a nation proud of its pattern of growth and development based in large part on the openness of its shores to people seeking an opportunity in the "land of opportunity."
>
> The quota system was set up in the immigration law of 1924. Many of its supporters saw this as a means of checking an Asian immigration invasion. But others adapted it to meet their own desires to limit the number who could come to this country from Southern Europe.
>
> We are a big nation with room—and a continuing need—to grow stronger. We can do this with the skill and ability of our native born and of those from other lands who wish to be a part of this great nation and to work with us in trying to fulfill its ideals.
>
> The time to worry about immigration is when people stop wanting to come to this country.

Seventy-two leading religious, civic, labor and social service agencies, members of the American Immigration and Citizenship Conference, jointly commended the President as follows:

We wish to endorse strongly the historic step you have taken in your Message of July 23 in calling for the elimination of the National Origins Quota System.

We have long urged the removal of this discriminatory aspect of our American immigration policy.

We are greatly encouraged and wish to express our appreciation for the outstanding leadership you are giving in this major field of human rights.